The Unmade Bed

The Messy Truth about Men and Women in the 21st Century

Stephen Marche

with commentary by his wife,
editor Sarah Fulford

SIMON & SCHUSTER

New York • London • Toronto • Sydney • New Delhi

Simon & Schuster
1230 Avenue of the Americas
New York, NY 10020

First Simon & Schuster hardcover edition March 2017

SIMON & SCHUSTER and colophon are registered trademarks
of Simon & Schuster, Inc.

For information about special discounts for bulk purchases,
please contact Simon & Schuster Special Sales at 1-866-506-1949 or
business@simonandschuster.com

The Simon & Schuster Speakers Bureau can bring authors to your
live event. For more information or to book an event contact the
Simon & Schuster Speakers Bureau at 1-866-248-3049 or visit our
website at www.simonspeakers.com.

Book design by Ellen R. Sasahara

Manufactured in the United States of America

1 3 5 7 9 10 8 6 4 2

Library of Congress Cataloging-in-Publication Data
is available.

ISBN 978-1-4767-8015-3
ISBN 978-1-4767-8017-7 (ebook)

To Sunny and Janet and
Bob and Geraldine

CONTENTS

ix

How Much Should a Man Speak?

I T is a well-established fact at this moment in history that men talk too much. They speak when they should listen, and once they start talking they go on and on and on and on and on.

Fifty years after the birth of feminism, when its promise of gender liberation seems closer and more distant than ever before, the word *mansplaining* has arisen to describe the sheer bulk of verbiage men foist onto the world. The word has followed the typical life trajectory newborn words take in the twenty-first century. Inspired by an essay by journalist and activist Rebecca Solnit, *mansplaining* started as an insider joke among journalists and activists, then spread to the *New York Times* "word of the year" list and the online *Oxford Dictionaries*. Its meaning expanded through the inflation of meme. So there were several variations. Some were serious (*whitesplaining, blacksplaining, ablesplaining*); some were not (*geeksplaining, momsplaining, Foxsplaining*). Then, as the word drifted into common usage, its meaning loosened. TV commentators pounced on White House spokesman Jay Carney for mansplaining the White House gender pay gap, but the slur failed to stick. Can you use *mansplaining* to describe any instance of a man explaining anything, even when he's answering a question you've asked him? The community of journalists who pioneered the word's adoption slowly began to pioneer its abandonment. There are plenty of overexplaining women, they pointed out, and occasionally men who speak are not doing so strictly to drown out the voices of women.

The word survives nonetheless because it describes a common social scenario so aptly. Solnit's inspiration was a man at a party who, on learning that she had written a book about film pioneer Eadweard Muybridge, lectured her on a recent book about film pioneer Eadweard Muybridge, which happened to be Solnit's book about film pioneer Eadweard Muybridge. It was yet another case of a man, confronted with a knowledgeable woman, displaying his own knowledge to the maximum—a dick-measuring contest where only one party has a dick. I first heard about mansplainers from a woman who started dating again after a divorce in her mid-fifties. On every date she was forced to endure mini-lectures on subjects about which she was an expert. I saw mansplaining in action just yesterday in the park. A young couple, in a cloud of marijuana smoke, lounging on beach towels they had spread in a patchwork equivalent of a picnic blanket, were playing chess, the man offering his opinion of each of her moves, right up to the point when she mated him. Immediately following his loss, he kept right on explaining the woman's moves to her.

For Solnit, these tiny but ubiquitous social interactions amount, in aggregate, to a politics of silence. In ways big and small, men have too much to say. "Having the right to show up and speak are basic to survival, to dignity, and to liberty," she wrote in *Men Explain Things to Me*. "I'm grateful that, after an early life of being silenced, sometimes violently, I grew up to have a voice, circumstances that will always bind me to the rights of the voiceless." But Solnit's larger political point is vague and nowhere near as urgent as the question of etiquette, of proper manners between men and women. In daily life, in the world in which men and women talk, the result of adding *mansplaining* to our vocabulary is that it might cause men who hear it or read it to think twice before explaining anything to a woman.

To take the example at hand, I am a man writing a book about men and women. I am thinking twice right now.

* * *

An empirical question first: Do men in fact explain things more than women? In her 2006 book *The Female Brain*, the American neuropsychiatrist Louann Brizendine claimed that the average woman uses nearly three times as many words as the average man. Other researchers disagreed immediately and vociferously. At the University of Arizona a group of sociologists attached voice recorders to 396 participants and found no statistical difference in how much men and women spoke. "The widespread and highly publicized stereotype about female talkativeness is unfounded," they wrote. (The stereotype in this case being that women, rather than men, have too much to say.)

In 2014, Harvard researchers used electronic monitoring and found that men and women spoke more or less depending on the size of the group and the setting. While collaborating on a work project, in groups of seven or fewer, women talked more and men talked more often. During a lunch break, women spoke more in larger groups, and men talked more in smaller groups. The problem in determining who talks more, men or women, when, where, and in what size groups, under what conditions, is a sub-problem of the attempt to measure social interactions reliably. The dynamic realities of human speech, setting and tone and situation, means that gauging which gender actually speaks more is nearly impossible. The human weather is too implacable.

A recent California State University study of email exchanges, which are easy to measure, found that women wrote more than men across a range of situations, in both work and personal messages. The researchers concluded that "electronic communications may level the playing field, or even give females an advantage, in certain communication situations." (The stereotype up for rejection in this case being that men won't shut up.) Likewise, almost every form of social media is dominated by women; 76 percent of U.S. women use Facebook, compared to 66 percent of men, and that divide more or less applies to the others: Twitter (18/17), Instagram (20/17), and Pinterest (33/8). The only exception is LinkedIn (28/27).

Who talks more has been one of the traditional battlegrounds in the gender wars. At the beginning of the feminist revolution, male reserve rather than male speech was the symptom of disease. In 1971 the sociologists Jack Balswick and Charles Peek published "The Inexpressive Male," an essay that became the basis of many thoughtful male responses to feminism. "As sex role distinctions have developed in America, the male sex role, as compared to the female sex role, carries with it prescriptions which encourage inexpressiveness," they wrote. For the men courageous and sensitive enough to recognize the import of the feminist revolution, the first requirement was expression: expression as release from frozen Stoic ideals and expression as the beginning of a considerate masculinity.

Men were encouraged to talk more, not less, particularly around women. In 1985 Michael McGill, author of *The McGill Report on Male Intimacy*, concluded, "Most wives live with and love men who are in some very fundamental ways strangers to them—men who withhold themselves and, in doing so, withhold their loving. These wives may be loved, but they do not feel loved because they do not know their husbands." The crisis was male silence and the solution was a cultural revolution, one that expected intimacy of men and sought to redefine the male nature of expression. Among the techniques for applying this new expressiveness were men's rights groups, consciousness-raising, cognitive-behavioral therapies, and just generally sharing your feelings and going on and on and on and on and on.

The men who tried to build a new model of male expressiveness were a vanguard. Jack Sattel, a sociologist right at the center of gender reinvention in the mid-1970s, understood the paradox of the premise right away. For men speech has traditionally been weakness. "Silence and inexpression are the ways men learn to consolidate power, to make the effort appear as effortless, to guard against showing the real limits of one's potential and power by making it all appear easy," he wrote. "Even among males alone, one maintains control over a situation by revealing only strategic proportions of oneself." The irony probably wouldn't comfort Solnit, but the man blathering on at that party is, in certain key respects, the end result of a conscious program to overcome gender restrictions, to make men give more of themselves.

The irony runs deeper than awkward scenes at parties. The entire discussion of mansplaining operates on the poor assumption that people explaining things are demonstrating more power. They aren't. Reserved speech has been the marker of masculine power for millennia. The strong silent type has an ancient pedigree. "Speak softly and carry a big stick" was Theodore Roosevelt's definition of U.S. foreign policy and, like so many descriptions of U.S. foreign policy, also a stand-in for fantasies of masculinity. During Robert Scott's doomed voyage to the South Pole, Captain Lawrence Oates knew that his frostbitten feet were slowing down the party as they struggled back to civilization. Before he walked out into a blizzard to die, he paused at the door and announced to his colleagues, "I am just going outside and may be some time." Scott wrote in his diary, "It was the act of a brave man and an English gentleman. We all hope to meet the end with a similar spirit." That spirit is manly brevity.

The Edwardian term for a mansplainer was *club bore*. In the novels of the period the men who talk too much are cold and cowardly. The club bore talks more because he knows less. Baldessare Castiglione in *The Book of the Courtier*, the guide to gentlemanly etiquette popular across Europe during the Renaissance, identified the phenomenon as early as 1528: "I will have our Courtier to keep in mind one lesson, and that is this, to be always wary both in this and in every other point, and rather fearful than bold, and beware that he persuade not himself falsely, to know things he knows not indeed." A gentleman keeps everything but his most certain opinions to himself: "Let him be circumspect in keeping them close, lest he make other men laugh at him." In the early sixteenth century men and women both were laughing at men who talked too much about things they didn't understand.

Reserved speech has been a defining feature of warrior culture since ancient Greece. Sparta permitted only the names of men killed in battle and women who died in childbirth to be remembered on gravestones. In 346 BCE Philip of Macedon sent messengers to Sparta with elaborate threats: "If you do not submit at once, I will invade your country. And if I invade, I will pillage and burn everything you hold dear. If I march into Sparta, I will level your great city to the ground." The Spartans sent back a single-word response: "If." Philip and his son, Alexander the Great, both chose to leave Sparta alone. Don't mess with men who are careful with their words.

* * *

Not explaining is always more powerful than explaining. The most powerful men and women I have known speak quietly and rarely, even those in publishing and journalism. Others have to lean in to hear them. Men don't make women voiceless and thus powerless; men make themselves voiceless and thus powerful.

The problem with *mansplaining* as a term is that men also have to deal with mansplainers. Mention you have a doctorate in Shakespeare, and they'll tell you everything they learned about *Romeo and Juliet* in junior high. Mention that you write for magazines, and they'll ruin your evening droning on about what makes a great magazine story, even though they've never written an effective email. The correct response to the guy who told Solnit about her own book is to laugh in his face. Laugh at him because he's weak.

I recognize that I am now mansplaining mansplaining. Behind that absurdity lies a despair that has haunted the feminist revolution from the beginning: the despair that men and women cannot understand each other. Despair over language is the deepest despair. If equality eludes us even in our words, how can we dream of justice in our bodies? The classic books of intergender linguistics have always betrayed a shared hopelessness, even in their titles: *Men Are from Mars, Women Are from Venus*; *That's Not What I Meant!*; *You Just Don't Understand*. "Male-female conversation is cross-cultural communication," Deborah Tannen wrote, depressingly, in *You Just Don't Understand*. Men and women need translators, like at high-power summit meetings.

If men and women are from different tribes or different planets, then we are doomed to a permanent stand-off. The battle of the sexes will be never-ending and the gender wars ongoing and irresolvable. But our language is failing us most of all when it comes to describing the state of gender itself. "The gender wars," "the battle of the sexes"—these are disastrous metaphors. We have used the word *war* to describe the historical process of men and women beginning to live together as equals. We have used *battle* to describe the advent of deeper intimacies and more just laws. The fate of men and women in the twenty-first century is toward equality: that much is certain. Women are gaining financial clout and political power consistently. In advanced economies misogyny and violence against women are declining consistently. In those successes lies the possibility of real recognition, a chance, after centuries of wandering the labyrinths of fabrication and disguise, for men and women to find one another. The hope of that discovery is turbulent, uncertain, fraught with unpredictable meanings. It is a messy, unmade hope. But it is real. It is happening. That hope needs promotion to the center of the debate. That hope is the fulcrum on which the world is turning.

We are entering the intimate wave of feminism, a wave that will have to include men, both as subjects and as participants. The language of conflict is no longer useful. The future can belong only to men and women together. The most vital, the most profound changes in the lives of men and women have occurred in their lives together: in bed, in families, in workplaces. Gloria Steinem's famous declaration is true: "Women's Liberation is Men's Liberation too." The opposite is also true. Men will have to do some of the explaining.

* * *

This book is the fruit of many confusions, both personal and intellectual—an attempt to reckon with the contemporary framework of gender relations in all their stunning flux, but also with the personal crises of my thirties: the sacrifice of my career for my wife's, the birth of my children, the death of my father. This book is half-argument, half-confession—a peculiar form for a peculiar moment.

My experience coincided maybe too conveniently with the general trends: the rise of women, the new fatherhood, the decline of patriarchy. But I am not alone. The statistically rendered trends, in all their cool clarity, bubble up into daily life as a welter of hot mysteries. The problems of men and women are the problems of flesh and blood, of giving birth and living and dying. They are the problems of sex and money and dreams and children and power. They require a philosophy of the nurturing womb and a philosophy of the stiff prick. The experiences came at me as the response of my body to the bodies that I love and the responses of my mind, always hopelessly late, to the responses of my body.

I have also included the responses of my wife, Sarah. The footnotes scattered through the book are hers. Sarah is an editor by profession and she edits almost everything I write; as she worked through this book, she started writing notes that I couldn't integrate into my own writing but felt I had to preserve. Without her perspective a part of the story of my own intimate life was missing. Read her notes as the positive inclusion of a female voice or as deliberate marginalization, as you wish. To me it was just another big favor I asked from my wife.

Whenever I read books in which a wife or a husband describes a marriage, I feel I'm being lied to. Maybe not intentionally, but inevitably. Marriages are mysteries even to the people within them. One side of the story will no longer do. The other side is always the revealing side anyway, the side that messes up whatever we may have thought we knew. Somewhere in that mess may be the real thing. That is my own messy hope.

Sex and Money and Dreams and Children and Power

———

ONE

—

The Hollow Patriarchy

After nine hours of labor, nine hours of a new person ripping her way into the world, my wife asked for an epidural and then the iPad so she could send a note to work. In my state of protective exhaustion I suggested that the time should probably be just for us and for the little body whose head was working its way through the birth canal. But it's hard to argue with a woman who's eight centimeters dilated. Besides, why not send the note? Soon enough the baby would be with us. The pause between the epidural and full dilation was the most calm we would know for months. Everybody is in the thick of it, in the mash-up of work and family, the confounding blur of everything, instantly, at once, the way life happens now. Why waste a moment?

While my wife and I waited for the baby to arrive—she on the iPad while I tried not to stare at the puddle of blood beneath her on the bed—we were waiting in a totally new reality than had greeted any generation before us. We barely noticed; the moment seemed utterly natural, despite its novelty and the slight tang of absurdity. The hospital was full of the gentle pings of the latest, most reassuring technology and the low murmur of sympathetic nurses, but no veil of hygienic modernity can disguise the brutality of what goes on there. My wife's vagina was on a raised platform for all to investigate, and she was still running *Toronto Life*. What was the note? A cover negotiation? A better lead to the second paragraph of some story or other?*

This quiet moment, utterly personal, was the result of a grand, very public revolution. A woman with a big job delivering a baby while her husband watched would have been inconceivable fifty years ago. Of all the grand political fantasies of the twentieth century, the various ideologies that dared to reconfigure humanity, and came and went, leaving behind the fetid stench of their failed utopias, only feminism has left a tangible legacy in everyday life. Even its limited successes have had vast consequences. Only now, only a generation after the major legal and political victories of the movement, are we reckoning with how vast, and often how hidden, those consequences are. Every aspect of life—financial, sexual, cultural, domestic, political—is undergoing unprecedented adjustment. The most lowly questions—Who will do the dishes?— run together with the grandest: Who will run the state?

The reach of lowly or grand questions seemed remote from the hospital room where Sarah and I waited for our daughter.

---

* In fact, I was telling the magazine's deputy editor that I might be offline for a while.

Nothing we had read mattered much one way or the other. The crisis was cosmic. Even love, or whatever other name you might care to give it, seemed a half-dreamed precondition to this moment, the arrival of a new soul. I could not stop looking at my wife—her hair, tucked behind her ears, glistening with the sweat of effort; her eyes scouring the screen in concentration. Sarah was iconic of the rearrangement we are living through, an absolutely contemporary but also ancient human condition: She was a mammal shaping the world.

* * *

I live a quiet life. I have a wife and a son and a daughter and a job and a house and a mortgage, and in the middle of all this quietude I am also in the middle of a world-shattering revolution, one of the most profound reevaluations of humanity ever undertaken, the redefinition of a core human distinction that has been in place for thirty thousand years. I am living the hopeful and uncertain fate of men and women in the twenty-first century.

Economics is the vehicle of that hope and uncertainty. The reality transforming the developed world, and to a lesser extent the developing world, is the rise of women to real economic power in the middle class. All the other changes—the changes that prepared the way for my wife on the iPad in the delivery room—follow in its wake. Companionate marriage, among other things, is an outgrowth of women earning a living.

Female professionals were one of the great novelties of the twentieth century. They define the economic order of the twenty-first. Since 1996 American women have earned more bachelor degrees than men. In 2012 they started earning a greater number of doctoral degrees as well. Of the top fifteen growth industries in the United States, twelve are dominated by women. The most recent Pew study of the state of the American family revealed the result of all that change: in 40 percent of all households with children under the age of eighteen women are the primary source of income. That ratio has risen continuously since 1960, when it stood at a mere 10.8 percent. It will not be long before the typical American breadwinner is a woman.

In a marketplace shifting rapidly to the manipulation of information, women have dived in headfirst, while men have watched timidly from shore. The pay gap survives, but ebbs. In 1980 women earned 64 percent of the median hourly wages of men; by 2012 the rate was 84 percent. Among those under the age of thirty, the rate is 93 percent. It's not the scope of the improvement that's impressive, but its continuity. The economic reality for women just gets better and better. The wage gap in the nations of the Organization for Economic Cooperation and Development (OECD), of which the United States is a member, has declined from 19 to 15 percent between 2000 and 2011. Women have increased their workforce participation in almost every country in the developed world since 2000. In the great middle, the twenty-first century will belong to women.

A formidable contradiction is starting to emerge as women close the economic divide, though. Economic equality should not be confused with parity; an increase in income or workplace participation is not the same as power. Men still hold the top jobs by an overwhelming margin. Women *earn*, but they do not as yet *own*. Just 172 of the 1,645 billionaires on the Forbes list in 2014 were women, and only twelve of those were self-made. The same gender divide at the very top remains ferociously persistent. Men have more say across a range of fields; for instance, they make up 76 percent of full professors in the United States and 66 percent of doctors and lawyers. And even though women have made significant gains in those last two professions—4 and 6 percent in a decade, respectively—at the peak of their earning, female doctors make two-thirds what male doctors do, and female lawyers are only 16.8 percent of equity partners at major U.S. firms. In the top tech firms women make up 15.6 percent of the engineers and 22.5 percent of leadership. Although it ranks sixth in the world, U.S. female board membership is a measly 12 percent. In supposedly liberal Canada, where I live, it's 6 percent, a national disgrace.

We inhabit a hollow patriarchy: the shell is patriarchal, but the insides approach the egalitarian. The contradiction generates strange paradoxes. Even women with servants and houses and powerful jobs, who possess hundreds of millions of dollars, consider themselves victims. And they're right. Women in the upper reaches of power are limited in ways that men simply are not.

The hollow patriarchy is political as much as it is economic. According to the World Economic Forum's "Global Gender Gap Report 2014," female representation in the world's democracies averages a mere 20 percent. The percentage of women in elected office in America makes for depressing reading: in 2013, 18.2 percent of seats in Congress were filled by women, and an even 20 percent of seats in the Senate. Only five governors are women; only twelve of the largest hundred cities in the United States have women mayors; only 20.8 percent of state legislators are women. The figures for women in other elected positions, attorneys general and so on, are roughly the same. And while female political participation is growing and has grown almost every year since 1979, when only 3 percent of members of the U.S. Congress were women, it is growing with painful slowness. At the current rate of expansion, women will reach political parity in Congress fifty-five years from now. And the situation is much the same in all the other Western democracies. When it comes to political power, "some countries are moving in the right direction, but very slowly," Saadia Zahidi, head of the World Economic Forum's Gender Parity Program, noted in an interview before their 2012 report. "We're talking about very small and slow changes."

Various men's movements, the most prominent of which is the National Center for Men, have emerged purportedly to provide a counterweight to feminism, but they are promoting an inherently absurd proposition. Power is still in the hands of a few men, even though the majority of men are being outpaced in the knowledge economy by every metric. The contradiction rolls both ways, inside and out. Masculinity grows more and more powerless while remaining iconic of power.

* * *

I began living the hollowness of the hollow patriarchy rather abruptly on the afternoon of April 12, 2007, in Prospect Park in Brooklyn. My wife called to say that she had been offered the position of editor in chief at *Toronto Life*. If she accepted the offer, she would be the first female editor of that publication, and at thirty-three, by far the youngest editor in chief in Canada. Her hiring represented, in its own small way, a generational shift.

And yet Prospect Park in the spring is not a place you want to think about leaving. The apricots were blooming. Relaxed families and groups of friends formed patchwork tribes over the rolling greenery of the East Meadow. Those urbane kids you find only in New York, the ones who know how the world works from about the age of four, chased dogs like kids from anywhere. I was thirty-one years old in 2007. Sarah and I had a beautiful son who was starting to walk; my second novel, *Shining at the Bottom of the Sea*, was about to come out, and my day job was teaching Shakespeare in Harlem, safe in the harbor of the tenure track at City College after five miserably lean years in graduate school. The call was an abrupt interruption to a carefully planned, painfully won setup. As a couple, as a man and a woman, we were faced with a stark choice: New York or Toronto?* My career or hers?

---

*Canada, I believed, would allow me to be an involved mom and have a rich career at the same time, while America, I believed, would have forced me to choose. When we lived in New York I saw what it meant to be a New York mother with a job in journalism. In New York office jobs no one leaves till 6 or 7 p.m. You take the subway to your tiny

I knew as I looked around the park that I belonged there. I belonged with my students in Harlem. I belonged with my New York publishers. My mind raced for a way to avoid the personal and professional disaster that moving back to Canada would entail. Could I stay here and visit my wife and son on the weekends? Could I convince my wife she could find work in New York, even though she didn't have a visa, even though she'd been offered her dream job? All my imaginary schemes collapsed as soon as they formulated because I knew they were really modes of mourning in advance for my lost futures, all the New York selves I would never become. City College paid me a little more than sixty thousand dollars a year, and my wife would make nearly double that in Toronto. Good hospitals are free in Toronto. Good schools are free in Toronto. This is what they call a no-brainer. Perhaps that was what was most upsetting about the decision to move back: that there wasn't

apartment, switching lines a few times, *if* the subways are working properly, which means that when you get home your kids are already in their PJs and they've had dinner. (A few years later the *New York Times* published an article about the importance of having dinner with your kids every night. I am pretty sure that the editors of that paper rarely eat dinner with their kids.) Getting your kids into decent schools involves lying, begging, borrowing, stealing. The challenges of New York parenthood often defeat even the toughest Brooklynites, who ultimately end up in Westchester or Montclair or Philadelphia if they are rich enough to afford the move. Why would you do that if you had an alternative? A lesson we learned firsthand: public policy can have a huge impact on quality of life. This is what Steve means by a "no-brainer."

much deciding. It felt like something that was happening to me, to us.

We left New York at the end of summer, and I restarted my life in the enlightened confusion of the new reality. Sarah and I took, in microcosm, the journey men and women in Western democracies have taken. She rose; she was responsible for the family's financial well-being; and she was a boss, with all the pressures and complications that accompany that role. As for me, I went from having about as traditional a marker of authority as you can find—a tenure-track professorship—to carting my son around the play spaces of Toronto before and after day care, on weekends when Sarah was still wrestling with her new responsibilities, and in the evenings when she was expected to show up at the self-important Toronto parties where nothing ever happens. I was suddenly my wife's husband.

* * *

Sarah obviously is an exception, even a pioneer, with all the usual bullshit that goes with that title. An elderly reporter, profiling her for a newspaper story, discovered she had a child and asked, panicked, "Where is he now?" As if Sarah just happened to forget his existence.*

---

*There are six years between our first kid, born when I was thirty-one, and our daughter because I needed that much time to figure out, practically, how I was going to be a woman with a "big job" while having a second child. During that time I talked to two other female editors in chief who had babies. I took each one out for lunch and, after swearing

In part the hollowness of the hollow patriarchy derives from the strange, almost unaccountable fact that gender politics at work and at home have diverged so widely that they now appear to be from distinct cultures. In the 1950s the patriarchy at work and the patriarchy at home were of a piece. The father was head of the household because he provided for the family, and the boss was head of the company because he provided work that provided for the family. For the overwhelming majority this mode of integrated patriarchy has disappeared. The days of Dad working all week and then, having fulfilled his duties, playing a couple or three rounds of golf on the weekend are ancient history. The new model of an equal household is triumphant. A 2008 Pew Research study titled "Women Call the Shots at Home" found that 43 percent of women made more decisions at home than their male partners did, and 31 percent of male and female partners equally divided decisions. (This bit of good news contains a further conundrum: Is making decisions at home a form of power? Would women's power in fact consist in

---

them to secrecy, asked for detailed accounts of how they managed their brief maternity leaves and how they returned to work and when. I took notes. They both advised me not to take much time off because I would end up working from home anyway, with a baby on my boob, not getting paid—they had learned that the hard way. So I created a business plan: After the baby was born I'd take six weeks off entirely, then go back to the office four days a week (with the proportional 20 percent pay reduction) for the duration of the summer. After Labour Day I'd go back full-time. I wrote it up and rehearsed delivering it to my employers. Then, and only then, did we stop using birth control.

making fewer decisions at home, in having less control?) There is no patriarchal "head of the household" in most households anymore. The family has changed and is changing further, while at work patriarchy remains intact and functional, surviving as a kind of lazy hangover, like daylight savings time or summer vacations.

The hollow patriarchy transcends mere culture; its process is driven by underlying economic realities. The rise of women is an aspect of globalization itself, and not the smallest. The "Shanghai husband" is a recent specimen of the burgeoning Chinese cities and is, more or less, what I became seven thousand miles away in Toronto. Shanghai husbands cook. They clean. They take care of the babies. They don't earn very much. "Many men joke fondly of their status as a Shanghai husband, oblique homage to the pleasures of domesticity," James Farrer wrote in *Opening Up*, his study of sexuality and market reform in China. In a 1999 episode of the Chinese television matchmaker show *Saturday Date*, the father of one of the female contestants approved of such a domesticated man for his daughter: "I myself am a Shanghai-style husband. I believe he also will be a Shanghai-style husband. I believe he has real feelings for our daughter. He will take care of her." These types emerge despite the obvious and ingrained sexism prevalent in China today, with state-run campaigns against "leftover women" (unmarried women twenty-seven and older), 117.7 boys for every 100 girls as of 2012, and no criminalization of marital rape. The Shanghai husband is a corollary of the Shanghai wife: the supertough, supersmart woman who kicks the shit out of foreign competition. I only wish I could have been as relaxed about my condition as my Chinese counterparts.

Idiosyncrasies of culture don't alter the basic economic trends at play. Insofar as any country participates in the globalized economy, it encounters the hollow patriarchy. The rise of the global middle class is the rise of women. Modernity is irrevocably feminist. Insofar as a country prospers, it prospers by way of women. In 2006, an OECD study demonstrated what common sense tells us: The countries where women flourish are the most stable, the most technologically advanced, the most peaceful, the richest, the most powerful. They are the countries that people in the rest of the world want to move to. Patriarchy is damn expensive. That's why it's doomed.

Exactly how expensive is patriarchy? A 2013 report from the International Monetary Fund described the labor market divide as a macroeconomic burden of the first order: "Raising the female labor force participation rate . . . to country-specific male levels would, for instance, raise GDP in the United States by 5 percent, in Japan by 9 percent, in the United Arab Emirates by 12 percent, and in Egypt by 34 percent." According to a Goldman Sachs study conducted in 2008, in the BRIC and N-11 countries (Brazil, Russia, India, and China and the so-called next eleven major economies), narrowing the gender gap in employment "could push income per capita as much as fourteen percent higher than our baseline projections by 2020, and as much as twenty percent higher by 2030." These forces are slowly but determinedly under way. Investment bankers are counting on them.

Politicians who are considering the role of women in the workplace and in society should recognize that they are asking themselves the following question: How poor do we want to be? Japan has recently announced some of the clearest and most direct attempts to smash the hollow patriarchy, both from above and from below, not because of a major ideological realignment or a widespread cultural shift but because of brute economics. Japan is patriarchal. Married Japanese women overwhelmingly stay at home. The country ranks a miserable 105 out of 136 in the 2013 Global Gender Gap Report. Roughly 1.2 percent of board members are female. In an attempt to budge these deep cultural imbalances Prime Minister Shinzo Abe has called on every Japanese company to have at least one female member on its board. And he has announced the building of 250,000 new day care centers. He is not undertaking these policies because he has suddenly realized that women are people too. He has realized that, given Japan's negative population growth rate and long recession, the country cannot afford to lose the productive efforts of its women.

The rise of women is a byproduct of capitalism, not of an intellectual movement or political activism. Feminism as an ideology has cribbed an emerging economic reality as a triumph of professors and activists. The rise of women is not a resistance to injustice; it is an unintended consequence of the internal logic of capitalism. Countries that insist on separating women from men for cultural or religious reasons are paying an immense price for it and will continue to fall behind as long as they maintain that separation. I suppose any country, any culture can waste its money on whatever it chooses. But keeping women down is a very expensive luxury.

Not that we should exaggerate the current state of the advancement of women. One hundred million women in West Africa have undergone genital mutilation—roughly six thousand a day. Amartya Sen's estimate of the number of "missing women of Asia," the girls who do not exist because of the cultural preference for sons, is a hundred million. The ratio of boys to girls at birth in India and China remains the same as it is in the Western world, 1.05 to 1.06, but the ratio of men to women is 0.94. The girls die off because, unlike the boys, they are denied access to food and medicine. Boys receive more education than girls in more than seventy-five countries. In global terms, we are by no means postfeminist. We are very much prefeminist.

Just as the majority of people in the world use firewood as their primary power source, so questions of gender relations, globally, are rather more basic than the contradictions in this book. The definition of domestic abuse, the use of sexual crime as an instrument of war, whether men have the right to rape their wives—these are the gender politics of most of the planet. Not that the discrepancy between the status of women in the first and third worlds means that the rise of women in the rich democracies is irrelevant. It is a vital instruction. The patriarchs have learned its lesson better than anyone. The liberation of women is the primary marker of modernity and prosperity. Therefore those who wish to be rich and modern will actively promote women. Those who justify their poverty by calling it tradition begin their assault on the future through the bodies of women. In the United States the first sign of traditional values is the restriction of women's control over their own bodies: the same groups that describe abortion as genocide actively discourage sex education or the promotion of contraception. Women's flesh must first be controlled: that control is synonymous with the old ways.

*   *   *

The economic underpinnings of the new reality between men and women shouldn't make us politically complacent, as if gender equality were going to take care of itself. The opposite: it shows how wasteful, how needlessly destructive keeping women from power is. The stakes are as high as they can be. How are we going to shatter this hollow edifice? How can we hasten its collapse?

The equality of women is spiritually and practically a flourishing of human potential. The hollow patriarchy keeps women from power and confounds male identity. It serves nobody's interests. And yet it may be harder to unravel than older modes of sexism. The struggles articulated by *The Second Sex* and *The Feminine Mystique* and *The Female Eunuch* were broadly oppositional: women against men, young against old, feminists against the existing power structures. The hollow patriarchy demands the negotiation of complex contradictions by men and women together, an infinitely thornier, more difficult process requiring compassion rather than force, empathy rather than outrage. Life between men and women is becoming less a battleground and more a labyrinth from which we need to thread a way out. The assumptions girding our lives are giving way. We need rearrangement rather than revolution. Rearrangements are quieter but they can be more profound. For one thing, the rearrangement of our moment is not just a woman's movement; it involves changing men and women together. For another, the rearrangement requires a more difficult and more nuanced politics than the gender wars of a previous era.

Revolutions require loud voices and slogans. Rearrangements require considered decisions, taste even. That's the bad news. The good news is that revolutions mostly fail and sometimes rearrangements work out.

*   *   *

The hollow patriarchy changes the nature of sex and domestic life and the raising of children. It infiltrates our dreams and our clothes and our music and our food. And, in the distance, though not the near distance, a reevaluation of the nature of power itself is coming. But before all those grand gestures, all those important overturnings of the nature of society and the gender roles it nurtures, there's the day to get through.

I enjoyed my time with my son when my wife couldn't be home. Long walks in the park (nodding to other dads), naptime (wasted online), a spot of lunch (grilled cheese and chicken noodle soup, or macaroni and cheese), cuddles (the best), snacks in the park (absolutely no nuts), nap (again wasted online), more walks (smiling less this time), more snacks (raisins and crackers), whiskey and water (for me), Dora the Explorer (for him), dinner, a hasty phone conversation with my wife about what was going on in the world of real people (not that I cared anymore), then bed (alone or together).

To hold a baby is to hold what matters: the point, the hope. Child care is restless labor; the total intimacy shared with another lump of flesh is no compensation for the utter loneliness of spirit that accompanies it. Driven from task to task, from moment to moment, everything in life seems adrift but also pressingly urgent. Leave your kid eating cereal while you run upstairs for a book, and he's shoved three Cheerios up his nostril and you have to suck them out, spitting the soggy snottiness into an unwelcoming palm. Check your email at the playground, and your son has run to squat in the road over an unfortunate worm that has modernistically dried in the middle of traffic. Pick a quarter off the street, and the kid is suddenly standing on the roof of a car. Ask yourself at the end of the day what you have accomplished and the best answer you can come up with is that not everything has completely fallen apart.

There remain the pressures of vanity and status. In downtown Toronto the school system is run by Vietnam-era draft dodgers and people who openly call themselves socialists—the progressiveness tends to expand into an unbearable holier-than-thou-off in Toronto—so I expected open-mindedness. But while Sarah and I were living out the new codes, the old codes remained very much in effect. The reaction to my unemployment and fatherhood-centricity was sharply divided along generational lines. Among Boomers classic gender stereotypes

prevailed. I had become "the woman" and my wife had become "the man." Mine was a case of straight emasculation.
Boomer men—and these were good guys, guys who considered
themselves forward-looking, guys who had lived through real
progress, who had seen the whole reality of men and women
overturned in their lifetime, who had helped bring about the
overturning—would vibrate with suppressed head shakes of
disbelief. And the women, kind women, women who were not
hateful, women who had steeped their radicalism in the tem-
pering waters of real life, would smile with amazement, eyes
glinting with the cruel pleasure that takes its fullest flavor from
righteousness. I was a living embodiment of patriarchy overcome, and they had contributed somewhat to my secondary
status.

Among people my own age the reaction was subtler. By no
means is my own story extraordinary. Well over half my male
friends have wives who make more money than they. Our family story nonetheless possessed a species of limited glamour. To
academic competitors and colleagues the fact that I had given
up a tenure-track appointment was like the charge of the Light
Brigade: glorious economic suicide. To others, giving up New
York for anything, even wife and child, verged on the inconceivable. Most friends and acquaintances roughly in my age group
at least understood the nature of the decision. They knew it had
nothing to do with politics or virtue or even my relationship
with Sarah. Hopping from city to city is part of twenty-first-
century life, and sometimes one person in a marriage has to
make sacrifices. Nonetheless I had become an addendum. One

of the lessons the contemporary marriage is teaching a lot of men—women have always known it—is that sacrifice is real. At first I thought through leaving New York that way, that I was doing what women had always done, sacrificing their career for their family and their partner's success. Another tormented thought pursued me: Would I have destroyed my career* for my husband if I had been a woman? If Sarah had had a tenure-track job in New York, would she have given it up?

The low point for me was a family dinner with my parents. They had their own new order to face up to, one in which their beloved son, whose expensive and seemingly ludicrously decadent education in various abstruse literary questions, they had supported and nurtured until it had miraculously ended in a real-life job. Which he had promptly abandoned. My father, who no doubt meant well, compared our situation to those of other academic couples he had known. "Every big career needs a wife," he said. So I was not just my wife's husband; I was my wife's wife. And to my father.

---

*Some context here. The truth is, Steve was always ambivalent about academic work. He loved teaching and was deeply attracted to the job security that a tenured position provides. But being a professor was never his dream. In fact he told me that writing his PhD thesis was an alibi—something respectable he could say he was doing—when he was actually writing novels. He encouraged me to accept the job at *Toronto Life* in part because it would free him from academic committee work, marking papers, publishing journal articles no one would read. Most significant, it would give him more time to write. Which is, in fact, exactly what happened.

I was also broke, one of the more precise terms in the English language. In giving up my middle-class income I found out how vulnerable you really are when you rely on somebody else financially. Let all men and all women heed the obvious lesson: Financial independence is all of independence. These were the dark days. Every marriage has them. "We've been married for twenty-five years," I remember my dad saying at my parents' anniversary. "Happily for twenty-two." I cannot recall exactly what Sarah and I screamed at each other, but it was about money. She had made promises about money she could not keep.* And I felt my powerlessness about money. We screamed at each other because screaming would change nothing. We were angry because we loved each other, and love and money had placed us in circumstances outside our control. Anger is its own form of intimacy. It kind of made it worse that I couldn't imagine divorcing her. Love was another way I was trapped.

As was sleeplessness. This story, and all of the psychic turbulence I am describing, should be understood to occur inside the condition of never sleeping more than a few hours at a time because the boy never slept more than a few hours at a time. The mood of desperate exhaustion permeated our lives like a

---

*Toronto isn't as expensive as New York, but it isn't cheap. After paying the rent and the bills and groceries, there wasn't much left over. My salary, which was pretty good, was still just one salary. I regret everything about this chapter of our lives and would do it all differently if given the chance.

chemical foulness. The most ferocious effect of sleeplessness is also one of the most difficult to see: insomnia sucks all the hope out of life. Insomnia makes it impossible to imagine that life will improve.

* * *

I remember, as a boy, waking up on a mattress in the back of a station wagon in a hospital parking lot in Edmonton, Alberta. My mother is a physician, who at that time delivered babies, and my father commuted to another city by plane every day. So, when she had to deliver a baby, a few times my mom had to put my brother and me in the back of the station wagon in the middle of the night and leave us in the hospital parking lot. Edmonton, Alberta in the winter is as dark and as cold as cities are allowed to be. Outside the station wagon, it could easily have been minus thirty or forty. But inside it was cozy. I loved the adventure. I didn't know that it was unusual for children to wake up in parking lots in the middle of the night. Later, I came to realize how my parents had clawed themselves, with single-minded ferocity, into the middle class through many such superhuman acts. Nor was their story atypical. My mother-in-law used to return home from her job as a radio broadcaster, feed two children, put them to bed, and then return to the office for a couple more hours of work. If it was like this for doctors and broadcasters, what must it have been like for factory workers? *Challenges* was the word my upwardly mobile parents used, I think. *Domestic challenges.* From my vantage point they seem like domestic impossibilities.

The rise of women has always been about assuaging competing demands of the domestic and professional spheres. The feminist movement, along with the rest of society, has assumed that taking care of children is women's work and a woman's political issue. The exclusion of men from the discussion of work and life is strange, because in heterosexual relationships the decisions about who works and who takes care of the children and who makes the money and how the money is spent are not made by women alone nor by some vague and impersonal force called society. They are decided by that blackest of black boxes, that repository of social mystery: the marriage.

The Pew Research study "Modern Parenthood," which came out in March 2013, found "no significant gap in attitudes between mothers and fathers." Working fathers are more conflicted than working mothers about work-family balance: 46 percent of working fathers worry about not spending time with their kids, compared to 23 percent of working mothers. The same report revealed the sharpness of changing attitudes toward the family. In the past decade the number of dads in America who stay home with their kids has doubled, up to 176,000. According to census data prepared for the *New York Times*, that number rises to 626,000 if you include part-time workers and freelancers who are primary caregivers, guys like me. In 2009, 54 percent of fathers with kids under seventeen believed that children should have a mother who didn't work. In a mere two years that number dropped to 37 percent.

For the Boomers and people older, the relationship between husband and wife, and the decisions about work made by husband and wife, are questions of power, and therefore political, ideological. Nobody asked me why we returned to Canada when we did. They knew it was money. In my experience, the modern marriage, and all of its decisions, and all the consequences those decisions have on the role of gender, boil down almost entirely to money. The conflict is no longer about the appropriate roles of men and women but the more general problem of the insane productivity demands of the contemporary workplace coming up against hunger for home life. The work-life problem belongs to both genders now. It belongs to everybody who needs money and has children and is subject to time.

The fact is, men can't have it all, for the same reason women can't: whether or not the load is being shared fifty-fifty doesn't matter if the load is unbearable. It will not become bearable once women lean in, or once the consciousness is raised, or once men are full partners, always, in domestic life. It will become bearable when decidedly more quotidian things become commonplace, like paid parental leave and affordable, quality day care.

If men's voices are absent from the conversation about family, we have, I'm afraid, only ourselves to blame. Those who speak loudest tend to be either members of the aforementioned men's rights groups or explicit antifeminists who long for a traditional family that bears little resemblance to the current reality. Men are not victims in this story, not helpless witnesses to their wives' struggles. And yet, while a chorus of women demands maternity leave, only recently, and only in the most progressive companies of Silicon Valley, have men started demanding paternity leave, and even then only for a few weeks.

A conversation about work-life balance conducted by and for a small sliver of the female population only perpetuates the perception that these are women's problems, not family ones. If you doubt that such thinking is still pervasive, see the recent op-ed in the *New York Times* about the effect of tax policy on working families, which contained this sentence: "Most working mothers who pay for child care do so out of their after-tax income." That's right: child care is a not a father's expense, or a family's expense, but a mother's. There are a hundred linguistic gaps between mothers and fathers in the tax code and in everyday life: stay-at-home mothers are parents; stay-at-home fathers are child care arrangements. Mothers are carers. Fathers provide care.

The residual prejudice explains why, despite the narrowing gender gap among millennials, both men and women feel that the narrowing is temporary. The gender gap for those under thirty is small, but it *feels* huge. The reason is the undeniable math of procreation: among millennials 59 percent of women but only 19 percent of men think "being a working parent makes it harder to advance in a job or career." Plus, 75 percent of millennial women and 57 percent of millennial men think that "more changes are needed to give men and women equality in the workplace." They are obviously correct. Twenty-three percent of American women return to work within two weeks of giving birth. In the United States the National Institutes of Health have rated only 10 percent of child care facilities nationwide as providing "high-quality care"; most are rated "fair" or "poor." And in every state the average annual cost of day care for two children exceeds the average annual rent. Not surprisingly, low-income mothers are far more likely to stay at home than are upper-income mothers. Such women are forgoing paid work because they can't earn enough money to cover child care. Although the situation is much better in Europe, across the twenty-seven countries in the EU, 26 percent of women with a child under the age of three who are working full- or part-time "report that suitable care services for children are not available or affordable."

Here is where, as we approach the end of the gender wars, we approach the limits of feminism as an ideology, because to concentrate on the needs of women is counterproductive. As early as 2008 Great Britain was already seeing the unintended consequences of maternity leave without paternity leave. "There has been a sea change on maternity leave and flexible work and we welcome that," said Nicola Brewer, chief executive officer of the Equalities and Human Rights Commission. "But the effect has been to reinforce some traditional patterns. The Work and Families Act has not freed parents and given them real choice. It is based on assumptions, and some of them reinforce the traditional pattern of women as carers of children." The struggle for maternity leave—the struggle for women—only creates another gender division, one that employers cannot help but recognize: young women have an inherent disadvantage due to their biology.

Only family leave solves the problem. Only by considering

the question from the perspective of the family as a unit can patriarchy be smashed. As long as family issues are miscast as women's issues they will be dismissed as the pleadings of one interest group among many. Fighting for the family is another matter. When gay rights activists shifted their focus from the struggle for their rights as an oppressed minority to the struggle to support their families, their movement achieved unprecedented political triumph. It is easy to have a career as an antifeminist. Force the opponents of day care support and family leave to come out instead against working families. Let them try to sell that.

The central conflict of domestic life right now is not mothers against fathers, or even conflicting ideas of motherhood or gender. It is the family against money. How do you hold the family together? Domestic life today is like one of those TV shows that reveal what goes on behind the scenes in show business. The main narrative question is "How the hell are we going to make this happen?" There are tears and laughter and little intrigues, but in the end the show goes on, everyone is fed and clothed and out the door.

* * *

I'm saying this as a man: day care saved my life. When my son was at day care, I could once again lift my head out from the miasma of domesticity. I could once again breathe and look around. I could once again write, and therefore earn. Eventually, David Granger, the editor-in-chief of *Esquire*, read something I'd written for the *Toronto Star* and called to ask me if I wanted a column in his magazine. I could take him up because of day care. Of all the privileges my wife and I possessed, the boy being in a safe place we could afford between nine and five was by far the greatest. Day care is not theoretical liberation; it is the real deal, for men and women.

The most progressive government policy in the past thirty years has been put forward by a male cabinet member of a conservative government. In February 2000 Norway's secretary of state for trade and industry, Ansgar Gabrielsen, set female board membership rates for companies on the Norwegian Stock Exchange at 40 percent. He explained:

> *The law was not about getting equality between the sexes; it was about the fact that diversity is a value in itself, that it creates wealth. I could not see why, after 25–30 years of having an equal ratio of women and men in universities and with having so many educated women with experience, there were so few of them on boards. From my time in the business world, I saw how board members were picked: they come from the same small circle of people. They go hunting and fishing together, they are buddies.*

When voluntary measures didn't work, Gabrielsen imposed quotas. The penalties included fines, deregistration from the stock exchange, and dissolution.

The rise of the "golden skirts," the Norwegian phrase for the new breed of female board members, has had no conclusive economic results so far, one way or another. A 2007

McKinsey report noted that having three women on an executive committee meant that a company outperformed its sector for return on equity by roughly ten percent. But a larger and later metastudy found "the relationship between female board representation and market performance is near-zero." Norway has not seen that kind of improvement, though there hasn't been a massive Norwegian financial collapse from the sudden arrival of inexperienced female board members either. Other countries are imitating Norway's success. France, Italy, Spain, and the Netherlands are instituting their own board membership quotas.

These supposedly women-friendly policies are every bit as valuable to men. The hollow patriarchy cannot be escaped until women hold legitimate power. We don't need a men's movement that takes sides in some phony gender war. We need a men's movement that understands the rise of women is a triumph for the species, one of the most unalloyed political goods ever achieved in human history, and who can acknowledge that this achievement does not require us to be ashamed of our masculinity. What good is a woman without pride to a man? What good is a man without pride to a woman? We need an understanding of gender that is in touch with the way men and women actually live—not in a state of war but in an often tormented, often achingly beautiful journey to intimacy.

* * *

The number of women in positions of power is steadily, though slowly, increasing, and it's possible that when women achieve a more substantial number of powerful positions, say a third of the Senate and the House and other bodies of representation, then their status as exceptions will evaporate and their rise to prominence will speed up. It's also possible that the progress will stall out. But the most likely possibility is more of the same: women underrepresented in political, economic, and cultural high places and increasingly equal or even dominant everywhere else. And the difference will continue to generate more of the turbulence we already live with.

Fury is the natural reaction to the hollow patriarchy. Young women's frustration at being kept from power is amplified by their obviously demonstrated competence. For at least three generations now women have shown beyond the doubt of any sane person that they can do whatever men can do. They are now better educated. They are evidently more dedicated. So the fact that they are kept from real power is even more bizarre and egregious. Aside from the limitations that the glass ceiling forces on individual lives, which are quite real, the hollow patriarchy renders femininity itself a marker of weakness, injustice, and humiliation. The struggle between Larry Summers and Janet Yellen for who would head the U.S. Federal Reserve—a struggle in which Yellen's "gravitas" was repeatedly questioned—happened in 2013, not 1963.

For men, or for the vast majority of men anyway, the hollow patriarchy is no more pleasant. They are expected to be powerful while having no agency. At the extremes, lost men decline into racism, neo-Nazism, explicit misogyny. These are the angry white men, subject to so much scrutiny. They are the ones who think their jobs have been taken away from them, the ones who long for the good old days that never existed. Everyone wants an excuse, I suppose. Everyone wants to play the victim if they can. In most men, however, the state of hollowness creates much more nuanced reactions: self-pity, confusion, light melancholy, the vagaries of an unplaceable, floating collective guilt, a melodramatic vulnerability, or, in the more fortunate, a sense of humor, an ironic sensibility. Mostly the hollow patriarchy produces silence. There is nothing less manly than talking about manliness.

* * *

While my wife was out at various events required by her position in the city, the boy and I had "guys' nights," the two of us watching hockey, eating Portuguese takeout with our rude fingers, often in our pajamas. Meanwhile, Sarah ate rubber chicken and listened to endless exercises in self-congratulation, introducing herself and being introduced to the billionaires, police chiefs, CEOs, local celebrities, and the rest of the powers that be.* Who was the "winner" and who was the "loser" in this arrangement is entirely a matter of perspective. Like a pagan, I worship what is newborn. I love a baby heart against my heart, breasts swollen with milk, tears, clipped nails, and the smell of

---

*This intense period when I was out three or four nights a week was pretty brief. After a year or two in my job I realized that going out one or two nights a week was just fine. Now I'm home for dinner way, way more often than not. I like it like that.

boys who have come inside from out of the snow. I would not trade the nights with my son for any other nights on earth, certainly not for Toronto hotel ballroom galas.

Simple cohort change is bringing a fundamental realignment of family dynamics with it. A 2011 study of millennials revealed that they are markedly more open to new models of the family, but that does not mean family is less important to them: 52 percent believe that being a good parent is more important than having a successful marriage. They have a greater sense of duty to their parents than Boomers or Generation X had to theirs.

Progressive tendencies dovetail neatly with their sense of family obligation. Women are going to have babies sucking their breasts at work.* Get used to it. They are mammals who

---

*Breastfeeding was, to my surprise, a great pleasure for me. My mother, a staunch feminist who spent much of her career as a radio producer, raised me to believe that the La Leche League was a group of deluded hippie evangelists dedicated to making working mothers feel inadequate. Then I experienced for myself the physiological oxytocin-infused high of a milk let-down coupled with the quiet intimacy of providing food through my body to my baby, and I was a convert. With our first kid I took a long maternity leave, which allowed me the time to breast-feed. With our second, born when I had more responsibility at work, I took a shorter leave, hired a nanny, and worked out a system that allowed me to breast-feed: I worked in the office in the morning (with a short break for a midmorning pump while I checked email on my phone), then I'd leave after lunch, drive like a lunatic across town, breast-feed my baby at about 2 p.m., then work the rest of the afternoon on my laptop at a neighborhood coffee shop and be home for a late afternoon, predinner feed. I now view the success of this crazy system as one of the great accomplishments of my life. I managed to

work. Men are going to leave the office in time to bathe their kids. Get used to it. They are mammals who work. Men even in the highest positions increasingly see time with their children as a nonnegotiable aspect of their compensation. Vice Chancellor Sigmar Gabriel of Germany, who is responsible for dismantling his country's nuclear power industry—a big job—decided to take Wednesday afternoons off to spend with his two-year-old daughter. He explained that the time away from his job served the professional function of keeping him aware of reality: "Otherwise we don't know what normal life is like."

Wanting a reasonable amount of time with the family is no longer a sign of weakness or lack of dedication; it's a sign that you're human and that you're aware of your humanity.* It's not

---

have a baby and breast-feed her until she was seven months old while maintaining a job that I love, all roughly on my own terms. I am aware that even the chance to attempt this feat is a privilege not available to most moms.

*An old college friend of mine who is a doctor told me recently that she is the "flex parent" in her marriage, a term I had never heard before. She works part-time in a medical clinic and has arranged her schedule so that she can be at home for her school-age daughters. Her husband is also a doctor, but his career is hospital-based and he works more hours per week than she does and has less control over his schedule. One of the best things about our lives in Toronto is that Steve is the flex parent. His work is no less important and no less demanding than mine (in fact he's on his laptop working constantly), but he can work anywhere at any time, which means that when one of our kids starts puking at school at 11 a.m., he can pick him up without causing

a sign of selfishness; it's a sign that you're a grown-up. To be a mammal and to be a human being is an impossible position, it should be pointed out. No gender politics, no politics of any kind, is going to solve the problem of being a body that wants to be more. No mere philosophy will ever solve the confusion of biology and aspiration and desire that is the massive human mess. Maybe at some point, though I don't see how, we'll reconcile being animals with the desire to be something more.

We pretend that family life is achievement and negotiation, a logic puzzle from an aptitude test. We fantasize that life is something built by the person living it, so that we may pretend that our fate is in our hands and that others are to blame for their failures. Control is, at best, a minor aspect of the human condition. Love is something into which we fall. The problem of work-life balance divides life into negotiable responsibilities, but there is no real balance, or rather the balance is a pose that

---

havoc in an office. Christopher Noxon, the husband of the superstar TV writer Jenji Kohan, calls that role "the domestic first responder." Anne-Marie Slaughter, in her book *Unfinished Business*, says she was the "lead parent" when she worked in Washington and her husband was in charge of her kid's day-to-day activities—playdates and dentist appointments and afterschool lessons. But what is the term for my parenting status, where I am the queen of the calendar and stay on top of the day-to-day needs of the kids—booking sleepovers, buying the shoes, scheduling camps, sewing up holes in Halloween costumes, hiring the babysitters for our evenings out—while Steve is the available one, who executes the plans and does more than his share of pick-ups and drop-offs?

is hard to hold. There is only falling down and getting up. There is loss and gift.*

*   *   *

In the meantime, children keep coming. In the hospital, after a rest that seemed much too long and much too short, the moment of crisis† rose on its own rhythm out of Sarah's womb. All the iPads were put away.

---

*The two loveliest presents Stephen has given me (in a lifetime of lovely presents): When I was in my early twenties I was struggling to write a magazine article about my beloved high school music teacher who was arrested and imprisoned for being a pedophile. I was working in a corner of our condo that was badly lit, and Steve bought me a simple silver desk lamp. He was saying *You can do it, I believe in you, this is important, your career is important.* A few years after I returned from studying Judaism at a yeshiva in Jerusalem, Steve bought me a tallit, my own prayer shawl. Steve's not Jewish, so to figure out how to buy the thing he had to consult my mother and travel with her to a super Jewish part of town and have lord knows what type of uncomfortable conversation with the store clerk. He was saying *Judaism is essential to you, I get it, and not only will I help build a Jewish home with you, but I will encourage this thing that matters to you.*

†Not a word I would use. In fact I was thrilled when my labor contractions started. Our first kid, six years earlier, was medically induced before my body was ready to go into labor—which resulted in thirty-six hours of fruitless contractions, many interventions, and ultimately a c-section. When my contractions started this time, I was past my due date, hoping to avoid a second c-section, and extremely eager to go into labor naturally. The rhythmic tightening around my abdomen was a source of joyful anticipation. I had a hard but happy

Our brief idyll of privacy suddenly filled up with a crowd: a midwife, a midwife in training, a senior surgeon, a junior surgeon, nurses galore. I've heard the saying that you're born alone and you die alone, but nothing could be further from the truth. Birth and death are public spectacles. The suffering joy of my wife as she pushed my daughter out of her was an event, a fascination. I could see, inside my wife, the head of another person.

But the pushing was not working. The head would roll up and roll back. It became clear after two and a half hours that my daughter's shoulder was catching on the inner crook of my wife's hip. So the doctors decided to suck my daughter into the world with a vacuum. Cheerful to the point of ebullience, the technicians of the flesh tinkered over my wife's vagina with what looked like a cheap bicycle pump. They attached. They pulled. They kept pulling while my wife pushed (from inside herself!), and the pulling and the pushing kept pushing and pulling until a lump of bloody life flopped up. A whole new body, a whole new soul, with all that it needs to live, thrust itself out of the womb like a god on a foaming sea of blood. The professionals who had seen it all a thousand times gasped as if it were the first time. A new little girl. In the hygienic roomful of hypermodern machinery, a bunch of apes moaned over new progeny. Life had begun again.

---

vaginal birth. The baby was born at 2 p.m. and by 5 p.m. I was home, with all four grandparents drinking bubbly wine. Come to think of it, the whole thing was about as far from a crisis as I've ever experienced.

TWO

The New Fatherhood

Twenty days after my daughter entered the world, my father left it. He died at sixty-four, unexpectedly, nowhere near ready. From my selfish little position in between death and life, I was glad he had a chance to hold his granddaughter a few times.

Death generates an amazing amount of paperwork. As I was dropping my son off at school a deliberately blank policeman's voice on the phone offered me no information other than an ominous instruction to bring my whole family to Toronto Western Hospital, which I did, where the same deliberately blank policeman told us that Dad was a corpse in the next room. He gave us an hour to pull our hair and weep—mammalian grief— then the paperwork. The family needed to approve an autopsy, since Dad had died on the street, without witnesses, right there in the open. His body had to be moved. Where? Under whose authority? Somebody needed to sign for his recovered belongings. Somebody needed to write the obituaries, which cost about eight hundred bucks per paper (that's how they get ya), enough to give me pause even when directly confronted by the clearest evidence I would ever receive that you can't take the money with you. It's almost as if the world decides to support mourners by the arrival of a tidal wave of busywork.

The first break I had all day was in the afternoon, on the walk to pick up my son from kindergarten to tell him that his grandfather no longer was. My father and my son had been close. The night before Dad died, they had been out for ice cream. The walk, the quiet decent houses, shaded by awkward trees, was freshly drugged by sadness and dread. How was I supposed to explain to my son what made no sense to me?

* * *

As the hollow patriarchy is slowly cracking, as the traditional male iconography frays and tatters, fatherhood has never mattered more. Having children has always been a major life marker, but the demise of other markers of masculine inclusion has left fatherhood with outsize importance. The old religious rituals gave way long ago. The postdynamic capitalism of the moment has taken away other methods of proving yourself. Making a living is principally a sign of good luck. Owning property is a sign of inheritance more than individual strengths. Combat itself is now gender-neutral. Only fatherhood remains indisputably masculine. Which is why, when you ask men when they became men, they will usually say it was when they became a father or lost a father.

The economic reordering of family life is a reordering of the iconography of the family. The two coincide; they are identical. The defeat of patriarchy will mean, before anything else, the building of a new fatherhood and a new motherhood. It's already happening. Since 1965 the amount of time fathers spend with their children has tripled. The rise of the stay-at-home dad—from 10 percent of caregivers in 1989 to 16 percent in 2012—is an extension of this aspiration. When working fathers see a man with a baby on the street in the afternoon, their first thought is "lucky bastard." And it's not only that dads love being dads more. Men who don't have children aspire to fatherhood more than they did before, more than women aspire to motherhood. In 2011 the largest study of singles ever undertaken found that young unmarried men want children slightly more than young unmarried women. Another study showed that men become more depressed and jealous than women when they don't have children.

Men want to be fathers more than ever before. They also fail at fatherhood more than ever before. The increased symbolic value of fatherhood has arrived in the middle of an accelerating crisis of fatherlessness. The number of American families without fathers has grown from 10.3 percent in 1970 to 24.6 percent in 2013; that percentage has more or less stabilized over the past five years, at the level of about a quarter of all families, which means that in 2016, 24.7 million children in the United States were fatherless. In the United Kingdom the number of families without fathers is increasing by twenty thousand a year, leading to the existence of "father deserts" in poor areas, where fewer than half of families include a father. Every country in the EU has followed this trend toward fatherlessness, as have Canada and Australia.

Only the most callow and naïve can see this development as some kind of fluid redefinition of the family structure. It's a social disaster. Fatherlessness as a condition has been linked with virtually every social ill you can name: young men who grow up without fathers are twice as likely to end up in jail; 63 percent of youth suicides are from fatherless homes, as are 71 percent of high school dropouts, 85 percent of children diagnosed with behavioral disorders, and 70 percent of all juvenile detainees. Fatherlessness correlates to higher aggression, lower achievement in school, significantly higher rates of delinquency, and increases in criminal activity. Psychoanalysts have identified the effects of "father hunger" in the night terrors of eighteen-month-olds.

In a 2014 study of more than 40 million children and their parents, researchers at Harvard examined the relationship between economic mobility and a series of factors, including racial segregation, income inequality, school quality, social capital, and family structure. Overwhelmingly family structure was the strongest connection. The crisis of income inequality and the decline of social capital are the subjects of wide-ranging, furious debates, and the quality of schools is the main subject of almost all local politics. But family structure matters more, much more. The researchers themselves were surprised at the strength of the connection: "The fraction of children living in single-parent households is the strongest correlate of upward mobility among all the variables we explored. . . . Family structure correlates with upward mobility not just at the individual level, but also at the community level, perhaps because the stability of the social environment affects children's outcomes more broadly." Though no studies with such breadth and vigor have been undertaken for the EU, the connection between fatherlessness and poverty has been well-established by researchers in all of those countries as well.

Again we see the limits of feminism as a political agenda in the face of the new realities of family life. "A woman needs a man like a fish needs a bicycle" may be true. But a kid needs a father like a fish needs other fish. (Exceptions are lesbian families, which show no trace of the crisis of fatherlessness. Why is unclear.) The figure of the father is more prominent because of rather than despite his widespread absence. Again the hollow patriarchy haunts us. The symbolic significance of fatherhood is at an all-time high, while real fathers, in the flesh, have gone missing. The rise of fatherlessness has revealed how intensely fatherhood matters. Fathers spending time with their children results in a better, healthier, more educated, more stable, less criminal world. Exposure to fathers is a public good. If the Harvard study is to be believed, and they looked at forty million children, having a dad is a surer sign of your ability to move up in the world than where you went to school or what neighborhood you're from. No wonder men want to show off their kids. Fatherhood is a clearer status symbol than a car.

The prevalence of the absent father distorts, in its turn, the perception of mothers. As fathers become symbolically vital but physically absent, mothers are exalted beyond all reason and degraded beyond all sense. The exaltation begins early, raising mothers to vertiginous, nauseating heights—they are the only ones who matter in childrearing and therefore are responsible for its results. I remember, while preparing for the birth of our son, reading* the various baby books whose sole purpose seemed to be to provoke, collectively, as much anxiety as possible. Do you sleep with your child in the same bed? She's going to grow up to be incapable of independence. Do you leave her to cry in her crib? She's probably going to be incapable of forming meaningful bonds. You don't breast-feed? You want your kid to have two dozen allergies? You do breast-feed? Don't you care about the future of women in society? Let your children go to the park by themselves, and the State of New York will

---

*As I recall, I read them. Steve didn't. I told him about what I read and blathered on about their conflicting expert opinions, but I'm pretty sure he never read any himself. Nothing made me feel more like a failure than William Sears's ubiquitous attachment parenting manual, *The Baby Book*. He's an evangelical enthusiast of back-to-nature practices like breastfeeding, co-sleeping, and baby wearing, which he argues can be scientifically demonstrated to be better for your kid, even though, if you do all of it in the way he instructs, it is hopelessly incompatible with having a career or, actually, a life. All my working mom friends read it religiously and then felt crummy about themselves for failing to measure up. Then we all read the *Harper's* article "The Tyranny of Breastfeeding" by the French philosopher Elisabeth Badinter and we all forgave ourselves and moved on. When I'm an old lady, I plan to look back at the Dr. Sears mania and wonder what the fuck we were all thinking.

prosecute you. Don't let them go to the park by themselves, and you're ruining their capacity for independence. Are you allowing them to be dirty? Are you not allowing them to get dirty enough?

It is impossible to overestimate the desire of the world to make mothers feel like failures. Perfection is not good enough. The guilt of the contemporary mother is like the guilt God should feel. And of course it's all so much pseudo-science. I remember dropping my son off at his first day of school and looking around the playground; I couldn't tell who was breast-fed and who wasn't, who was raised by attachment parenting and who wasn't, who drank organic milk and who didn't. Only one distinction flared up: kids who were loved enough and kids who were not loved enough. The kids who were loved enough had love to give. The kids who weren't could never spare any.

The exaltation of the mother as the icon of all parental responsibility is a natural response to the crisis of fatherlessness. Increasingly, without the presence of a mother there is no family at all. Without single mothers the streets would run with feral children. And yet the single mother is the preferred scapegoat for the world's remaining scolds. Political parties have built major affiliations on the simple premise that the state should give less to single mothers. Impossible sacrifice is expected of them, and many want to make it more impossible. Attacking single mothers is the moralists' alternative to blaming poor people for their poverty.

On the other edge of the social spectrum, to be a professional mother is to have to dig a huge hole, then throw yourself in. Working mothers, required for a modern economy, have to endure the assumption that they are failing in both roles: a woman who works cannot possibly be taking care of her kids properly, and a woman with kids cannot possibly be dedicated to her job. Successful women have made a minor industry out of extolling and celebrating their exhaustion. There is a strange idea stalking us, that motherhood is a space for expected achievement rather than a biological state of being.

And, almost needless to say, in all the pregnancy books and child-rearing books, men are there to make money and hold the purse. We don't expect much of a dad—an insulting but luxurious position in its lazy way. One of my editors at *Esquire* remembers returning home from shopping in the East Village, toting a bag of groceries and fronted by his newborn son in a pouch carrier. "You're a good father," two ladies passing by muttered to him. "I was buying fucking milk" is how he put it to me.

At the heart of the new fatherhood is a somewhat surprising insight: men, as men, are worth something. The epidemic of fatherlessness and the new significance men place on fatherhood point to the same clandestine truth. The most startling conclusion of the research into fatherhood may be simply the power of their brute presence. The Harvard study of upward mobility does not say that *good* fathers are the strongest correlate. It says that family structure is. Being there—mere, dumb being—is the difference. Presence is what matters.

On the walk to my son's school a few hours after my father died, the numbness started to wear off and the newness to seep

in. I had been drifting. The hospital hallways, the car trips between our house and my parents' apartment, the phone calls
to relatives—they had all possessed the stasis of the unreal. But
now the surface of the street suddenly burned with change;
the leaves flickering in the bright sunshine shook with the fact
that they would soon tumble; the cars trembled with approaching obsolescence. "Change is the only constant" is a wonderful
premise for a bumper sticker. People are entering and leaving
the world every moment. But the consciousness of this obscene
fact is unbearable.

I needed my father to advise me how to deal with his death.
I needed my father to tell me how to tell my son that he wasn't
there anymore. I needed to hear, as I had heard so many times
before, his slow intake of breath, a half-sigh, as he considered
whatever question I had brought him. I needed to see his eyes
closed in thought, his thick hands folded together in momen-
tary meditation. I needed to see him thinking up solutions to
the problems at hand, maybe more than I needed to hear the
solutions themselves. He had experience and he had remained
cheerful about it—a powerful combination, and no mean at-
tainment.

His importance in my life had never been more vivid. We
rarely agreed about politics or anything like that, but we were
both smart enough to recognize that we weren't supposed to.
He grew up in poverty, managed to educate himself through
the military, became very interested in poetry, was a venture
capitalist and then a professor, walked to the eighty-eight Bud-
dhist shrines on the island of Shikoku in Japan. His own father

died when he was eight, and yet he managed to turn himself into a man of the world.

How would I do?

* * *

"The memory of the dead" is such an imprecise phrase. It offers an illusory impression of solidity, of fixity in space and time. It's also strangely singular. Memories of the dead are polymorphous: a photograph of sharing a bath with Dad and my brother when we were kids, the orange at the bottom of the Christmas stocking, a bruised thumb from splitting wood, a long story he used to tell about the front gate at Royal Military College that ended with the punch line "Bird poop, sir," the explanation of how rooks and bishops move on a chessboard. The memory of the dead is a residue of intimacy, a swirling dust that kicks up in your chest and scours it until the dust rushes out into the world like a whirlwind and belongs to nobody. Death is not the end of intimacy, that is for sure. In a way, memory is the most intimate of interactions. A working definition of intimacy is a memory forming in the present.

The switch that had flipped as I walked to my son's school was binary. My father had always been there when I needed him, right up until that moment. The street that I was walking down was a street I could not walk down with him anymore. Just before I arrived at my son's school, I ran into my wife's cousin, a good guy of the sun-bleached, laid-back variety whose own father had recently died. He had the misfortune to ask "How you doing?" to a guy whose father had just died unexpectedly. I told him. Instantly he stuck out his hand and shook mine. It was weird. We laughed at its weirdness at the time. He later told me he was embarrassed by the gesture, but I came to realize it made perfect sense. He was congratulating me. That day, on that walk, I had become a man.*

* * *

The discrepancy struck me even as a child: that my dad was not like the dads on television. He represented to me—he still

---

*Those first few months after my father-in-law's death, with a newborn in the house, a bewildered and grieving family, and a sweet little six-year-old boy jumping around in the midst of it all, were almost too much to bear. We lived in a hot, painful stew of tears, breast milk, baby poo, and laundry. During that period my family was tended to, largely, by a raft of professional women, friends, neighbors, and family members—lawyers, doctors, professors, journalists. Having big careers did not stop them from taking care of us. No wonder women so often complain of burnout! Something I learned acutely during this period: you never forget the kindness of people who help you survive a personal tragedy. Every sympathy card matters; to this day I can quote lines from some of them. You remember every loaf of banana bread hand-delivered to your door, every casserole and jar of soup found on your porch, every bottle of scotch dropped off. This essential life-sustaining work is mostly done by women (with the exception of my wonderful cousin John, who baked and cooked and kept coming around). Why mostly women? Is it because women are better at anticipating what a distressed family needs? Is it because women learn how to hand-write cards and cook lasagna (even while they are earning their MBAs)? Anne-Marie Slaughter argues that in the next stage of the feminist revolution, men will become caregivers too. I suspect this will take a long time.

does—an open masculinity, a way of being a man without being boring or intentionally stupid. And he had found that path largely by himself. I suppose he was eccentric, although really he was interested in things and unafraid to be interested in them. If he suddenly cared about origami, he would study origami. If he suddenly grew passionate about D. H. Lawrence, he would go and read all of D. H. Lawrence's novels. This was not what dads were supposed to do. They were supposed to want their usual chairs and not to be bothered.

The standard family on television today—and it's hard to think of any exceptions—consists of a hypercompetent woman and the dumb slob she married. The fathers come in two principal varieties: Mr. Mom and Fat Pig. The ur–Fat Pig is Homer Simpson, a man who worships a waffle stuck to the ceiling, but the purer expression is probably Peter Griffin from *Family Guy*, the farting, mentally handicapped narcissist whose subsidiaries amount to a billion dollars of television production. The Mr. Mom type is defined by the defeated, awkward, confounded Raymond on the ironically titled *Everybody Loves Raymond*. The most popular shows of the past thirty years have all been about family, and all have an idiot dad at the center. Every season produces its crop of imitators.

These cultural stereotypes are now starting to crumble; fatherhood is changing so thoroughly that they have to. The clearest evidence that the bumbling father is doomed comes from advertising. In 2011 a Huggies spot claiming that their diapers "could even survive dads" was pulled when it provoked outrage. Dads attacked on Facebook first, then a small group of activist dads—let us pause to consider the mere existence of the phrase *activist dads*—petitioned the company directly. Huggies pulled the ads immediately and went to the Dad 2.0 conference to make the most of their apology. Now advertising is swinging the other way. Volkswagen ads show concerned fathers asking, "Is it safe?" Drew Breese, star quarterback of the New Orleans Saints, is shown rubbing Vicks VapoRub on his real-life son's back. The 2015 Super Bowl was dubbed "the Daddy Bowl" because so much advertising shoehorned so many companies into the aesthetic of modern fatherhood. Nissan played "Cat's in the Cradle" over racing footage.

Advertisers have realized that men who consciously think of themselves as fathers and are passionate about that role represent a sizable market. Still, the engaged father remains an alternative form, a peculiarity worthy of op-eds. The cool dad retains all the cultural apparatus that status implies, with self-consuming, inherently narcissistic, demanding poses that co-opt and then mock. That double process certainly greeted Neal Pollack's *Alternadad* when it was published in 2008. When *Kindling Quarterly*, a journal for design-conscious fathers, launched in 2013, I knew I was supposed to make fun. I mean, the first issue had a recipe for pumpkin gnocchi. But I didn't. Fatherhood is one of the truly binding connections between men, no matter what aesthetic cloaks it. If you've ever wondered why new parents are so unbearable to be around, especially for people who don't have kids, it's because they are overwhelmed by the strength of their personal transformation. Like teenagers who've lost their virginity, new parents have been inducted into a secret, and, at least for a while, that secret seems to be the whole of the world. Men who are fathers share in that secret, no matter their other distinctions.

* * *

One of the most surprising, intriguing possibilities of our moment is that the family, despite its complete revaluation and the collapse of its traditional structure, has lost none of its power as a social institution. The old vision of the family—Dad works, Mom stays home with 2.3 children—has vanished into history, or rather its dominance has. The nuclear family is now one aesthetic choice among others. A huge array of options and modes of family life have emerged. Those who prophesy the demise and decay of the family as a social institution have not been paying attention. According to the National Center for Health Statistics, the U.S. divorce rate doubled between 1940 and 1981, but then fell by a third from 1981 to 2009. A new set of family values is emerging that is fiercer, in its way, than the dull societal expectations that came before.

The most obvious shift is the expanding acceptance of gay marriage. In terms of sheer velocity, the rise of gay marriage is a nearly unprecedented political victory, one that has created some oddly jarring juxtapositions. President Barack Obama himself, that icon of hope and change, was "evolving" as late as May 2012, and he finally came around only because Vice President Joe Biden forced his hand. A few months later Obama and the Democratic Party phrased the question of same-sex marriage as a civil rights struggle. Less than two years after that the CEO of Mozilla was pushed out of his company for having financially supported California's Proposition 8, the 2008 ban on gay marriage. Meanwhile, in Russia and Uganda explicit homophobia has become a means of resistance to the decadence of Western democracy. The haters have seen the same truth everybody else has: acceptance of homosexuality, like the promotion of women, is a sign of modernity, plain and simple.

No one has really figured out why the support for gay marriage has risen so swiftly in the United States, from 27 percent in 1996 to 55 percent in 2014, finally resulting in the decisive 2015 Supreme Court victory in *Obergefell v. Hodges*. One theory for the suddenness of the rise, and not a poor one, is simple exposure; when you have a lesbian couple living down the block, their kids playing with your kids, and you see them grocery shopping, being as boring as hell, it is hard to want to destroy that evident and substantial love because of some ethereal morality. A Pew Research survey in 2013 on the growing support for gay marriage found that 32 percent of those who changed their minds did so because they knew someone who was gay, the most common reason by far. One hopes that declining ignorance and common sense also played a role. Thirty years of research by the American Academy of Pediatrics has shown that children's well-being is barely affected by the sexual orientation of their parents. Only the willfully ignorant can accept the argument that homosexuals are incapable of forming healthy families.

But the power of argument is limited. New family values do

not emerge because people begin thinking differently. Compassion and reason are unfortunately nowhere near powerful forces in this world. Instead the new tolerance toward gay marriage comes from a new consciousness about the family, an aesthetic turn that is intimate as well as political. No longer is family something you do because you're a woman and he's a man and, hey, you have to start fucking sometime and the paperwork is easier. The new family is a mode of lifestyle construction.

The acceptance of gay marriage would not have spread so rapidly if straight marriage were not in the middle of its own upheaval. As straight sex begins to include acts that were once illicit, the capacity to hate others for performing those same acts inevitably erodes. Along with the physical abjection, the morality it underpinned vanishes. How can you condemn a gay couple for what you're doing? We can't accept others without accepting ourselves first.

* * *

The straight family, as a mode, as a cultural practice, increasingly resembles, and aspires to resemble, the gay family. They have moved from pariah to paragon in a generation.

I understand this more-than-tolerance is a luxury of my time and place. Toronto in 2015 is an exception; the premier of the province is a lesbian grandmother, after all. When I think of gay marriage, I do not imagine an abstract category. I think about a family I know with two dads and a bunch of kids, all living right out of a children's story of the fancier sort, in a big old house in what looks from the outside like a nonstop caper. The kids originally come from around the world. A raft of nannies (what is the collective noun for *nanny?*) maintains order and fills in various blanks that arise in various schedules. The family is miraculous.

Or, rather, my outsider's fantasy of what is, no doubt, their own complex struggle finds them miraculous. Not that their evident happiness, even in my imagination, means anything more than the dads' good fortune and hard work and strength. Plenty of gay families, I assume, are miserable. Their stories possess attractive qualities nonetheless, vividly attractive. Here are people who have built their family out of determined love and who have arranged their domestic life out of personal inclination and rational discussion, not inherited, discredited gender roles. They have made their own traditions. They have marriage without all the bullshit between men and women. They have marriage on the terms that suit their particular needs and desires. Isn't that what we're all looking for?

Obergefell v. Hodges was far more revealing about the state of straight marriage than the state of gay marriage. The conflict was not between competing interpretations of the U.S. Constitution but between competing feelings about intimacy and dignity. In the Supreme Court's majority verdict, Justice Anthony Kennedy made a play for being recited at wedding ceremonies:

No union is more profound than marriage, for it embodies the highest ideals of love, fidelity, devotion, sacrifice, and family. In forming a marital union, two people become something greater than once they were. As some of the petitioners in these cases demonstrate, marriage embodies a love that may endure even past death. It would misunderstand these men and women to say they disrespect the idea of marriage. Their plea is that they do respect it, respect it so deeply that they seek to find its fulfillment for themselves. Their hope is not to be condemned to live in loneliness, excluded from one of civilization's oldest institutions.

The dissent, from Justice Antonin Scalia, took a decidedly alternate view of the nature of marriage: "Who ever thought that intimacy and spirituality [whatever that means] were freedoms? And if intimacy is, one would think Freedom of Intimacy is abridged rather than expanded by marriage. Ask the nearest hippie." For Scalia marriage is an abridgment of intimacy, a restriction of the possibilities of human communion, a conclusion to the freedom of love. *Obergefell v. Hodges* revealed a whole range of oppositions crackling through straight people's understanding of their marriages. Choice against duty. Engagement against obligation. Respect against traditional roles. But one side in all these oppositions is winning. Choice and engagement and respect are more powerful than duty and obligation and tradition.

Support for gay marriage is as good a metric as any to see how quickly the new vision of the family is replacing the old one: at about 2 percent a year. Fast. More than fast. The change is coming suddenly and forever.

* * *

Someday the Republican Party is going to have a meeting in some Howard Johnson in North Carolina and realize that the people who share their most vaunted values—"personal responsibility," "the importance of family," and "liberty in the pursuit of happiness"—are gay people. They will then have to ask themselves many perplexing questions about why they have invested so much time and effort deliberately and loudly despising people who believe what they believe.

A few Republicans smell an opportunity in the new research on the family but don't quite know what to do with it. In January 2014, in a marquee speech on poverty, Senator Marco Rubio of Florida put the family at the center of his economic policy: "The truth is, the greatest tool to lift children and families from poverty is one that decreases the probability of child poverty by eighty-two percent. But it isn't a government spending program. It's called marriage." Republican preoccupation with family values is nothing new, but the economic motive is. And their math, this time, is correct. They have so far used their new appreciation of the crisis of fatherlessness and the rise of the new family values to do little more than launch broadsides against various something-nothings of culture and to reject the idea that public policy can have any effect on the family whatsoever. For them the new fatherhood is mostly an excuse for inaction.

If Republicans looked more closely at the mechanics of fatherlessness they might gain insight into a host of policies. For instance, immigration reform is vital because the policies in place today destroy families. At the current rate 1,100 undocumented immigrants are deported each day. By one estimate deportation will separate 152,000 children from one of their parents. Now that we know how deeply family structure matters, destruction of families on such a scale can only be considered a kind of cultural genocide, just as the drug war, by incarcerating African-American men at four times the rate of white men for negligible possession offenses, amounted to cultural genocide. A few Republicans who actually deal with the fallout of government policies on families, like governors Rick Perry and Chris Christie, have recognized the cost of these disastrous policies. Both have spoken about ending the drug war.

Democrats don't want to hear about fathers much either. President Obama could approach family structure only tangentially. In February 2013 he announced a private-public partnership, My Brother's Keeper, a tentative first step in addressing the problem of minority boys, who are the most vulnerable. At the announcement Obama said, "Nothing keeps a young man out of trouble like a father who takes an active role in his son's life." It's "American families" boilerplate, of course. But the data show that it's actually true as a matter of policy, and not only for minority boys but for all boys. My Brother's Keeper was a gesture, an important one—possibly a trial balloon?—but a small one. A family-based approach to inequality has the aura of a host of outmoded prejudices many on the left have spent their entire careers fighting against. They prefer to focus on the traditional approaches of grievance politics, with the emphasis on class and race. But the most powerful way to alter those inequities is through family structure.

Obama understood the craving for the fatherly bond perfectly, instinctively. He ate dinner with his family almost every night; no doubt he enjoyed the time with his girls. But he must have understood how much that gesture represents the ideal of a new masculinity. He himself embodied the transferred status of fatherhood: once the president was the Father of the Nation; now the president must just be a father.

The changes the politicians are trying to gauge are far more profound than those that can be reflected in mere policy shifts. The subterranean rivers are churning. The ancient conception of the family as a social reflection of a biological distinction—man and woman united by an imposed code of rights and obligations—has given way to an idea of the family as a contract of equals, whose arrangements reflect the diversity and particularity of all human desire. The family is shifting from social arrangement to work of art.

* * *

A single small but vital fact distinguishes men of the past fifty years from all other men in history: most of us see our children being born. I remember my mother telling me over coffee one afternoon that Lamaze was the most important moment in gender relations over the course of her lifetime. It wasn't the publication of *The Feminine Mystique*. It wasn't the Pill or *Playboy*. Women have knocked down many walls to get into many powerful places. Men knocked down the wall to the delivery room. Up until the mid-1960s the mysteries of birth were strictly the preserve of women. Then, suddenly, they weren't.

Men insisted on being with their wives as they gave birth and with their children as they came into the world. This single act changed the position of men in relation to women and to children and to domesticity itself. It was a fundamental shift in the gravity of family relationships.

The old fatherhood was a series of unexpressed assumptions. The new fatherhood requires intelligence. It requires judgment. The new fatherhood is messy. It has to be. In the face of this messiness there are men, and not just a few, who retreat into fantasies of lost idylls, worlds where men were men, whatever that might have meant. Only the truly lost man would want to return to his grandfather's way of life, to the bad food, the boring sex, the isolation, to being financially responsible for a family and then never seeing them. The new fatherhood is a huge gain for men, the chance for a whole new range of pleasures and agonies, a fuller version of our humanity, a deeper intimacy.

For women the canard of failure on both fronts promises to vanish. Experience is forcing the vanishing. I never once thought of my mother as "absent" because she worked. Studies from as early as the 1950s have consistently shown that the children of women who work have no significant differences in attachment to their parents, in psychological health, or in achievements at school; there are not even significant differences in the amount of time stay-at-home moms and working moms spend with their kids. It makes sense: there's only so much time parents and kids can stand to be with each other.

Of all the grand upheavals between men and women over the past two generations—the sexual revolution, the rise of women in the workplace, and the rest—the new fatherhood has been the easiest for men. Despite no historical examples of male nurturers, almost no literature of the macho caretaker, men took to the new fatherhood in all its fleshiness and complication without much struggle, indeed with relish. Today the overcaring father is a mockable cliché; you've seen them comparing stroller models at the playgrounds, giving baby a bottle in a bar during the Final Four, discussing the latest studies on the merits of early music education on "executive function." Witnessing birth was the beginning. The new father is an engaged father by instinct. The new father holds his babies. He bathes them. He reads to them. The new father knows that the role of the father is not merely to provide. The role of the father is to be there, physically and in spirit.

Not that I remember all the times my own father was there. Who could remember all the times he waited in the middle of winter in Alberta, reading a day-old newspaper in the car, for me to finish my piano lesson? Who can remember the money he gave me? Or the advice? Oblivion is not ingratitude. His presence was auratic, a warm glow, the weight of a thick hand on my shoulder, the heaving of his chest while he napped. The aura is identical to the inexpressible sense that he loved me. It was known to me. But this did not need to be said. Not often anyway. It was not said often enough. As I went to pick up my son, I remembered my father's hands, pinched lovingly by the golden band. Childhood is filled with hands at eye level. Despite all his hands had done, despite their various caresses, I remembered them at rest.

*   *   *

The day Dad died I brought my son back to the house and sat him down in the living room with his mother. I told him his grandfather was dead. He wanted to know if that meant he would never see him again. I said yes. Then he started to weep. The lesson was harsh for a six-year-old: people are here, and then they're not. He threw himself into my arms. I was his father. And that meant, right then, that I was there. I was there for my son. I would be there until I wasn't. And that was enough.

THREE

—

Straight Camp

Afew weeks after the birth of my daughter and the death of my father, my mother gave me my grandfather's war watch. Curled in crepe paper inside an empty shoe polish can in the back of a cupboard filled with other family ephemera, blackened and defaced by time and indifference, the thing looked more like a crust of rotten bread than machinery. I was grateful to have it. My mother was grateful to give it away. I wanted things that lasted. My mother wanted to give away as much as she could. Grief was rummaging through us in opposite directions. Also, small point, I needed a watch.

If my father was an icon of the changes of a previous generation, my grandfather was an icon of the way men used to be. He fathered and raised seven children and supported his family by working the railroads and hunting and fishing and tending to a garden with neat rows of staunch corn and feathery lettuces, thumb-thick beans, and candy-sweet carrots and with boundless rhubarb patches whose crisp stalks I was

free to rip and chew. My memories of him were mostly of the
summer vacations I spent on the family homestead in New
Brunswick, memories of a shirtless boyhood, my grandfather
egging on the boxing matches between me and my older cousin
James, who had a foot in height on me and two feet in reach
(although my grandfather admired my scrappiness—I could
take a punch), or leading us to the camp tucked onto the edge
of the Canaan River to fish for tiddlers with corn niblets that
reeked of the tin they came in, or driving the pickup to the
local dump, suppressing our gag at the reek, to pore through
the fly-rifled piles. Once we found a Swiss Army knife with
only a few of the attachments snapped off. James, entitled as
elder, kept it.

They were sunny memories, memories of the freedom a city
kid enjoys with country relatives, but I knew, even then, that
shadows followed by grandfather. I could sense their darkness
exactly because they were so scrupulously kept from me by my
mother, by my grandmother, and by my grandfather himself.
His means of retreat was rum, which he camouflaged in
pineapple juice. The source of his darkness, I knew, was The
War. He had flown only once since 1945, when he traveled
across the country to see me, just born. He had to get so drunk
to get on board nobody ever suggested he fly again.

When my mother handed me the rusted, abandoned war
watch, it fit into my hand like something the hero at the beginning of a fable might receive, an amulet or a clue. I took it to a
fancy jeweler in downtown Toronto, where a devoted, monk-
ish master craftsman, accent from somewhere in the Cauca-

sus, undertook its restoration the way engineers undertake the
bridging of rivers, with a kind of basic human determination to
overcome the forces of nature. He soaked the face in a solution
for three months. He ordered parts from Switzerland, which
took half a year to arrive. He fiddled. He rebuilt. Nearly a year
later he handed me the burnished machine with a lesson on
how to wind it and what amounted to a massive compliment:
"This is a good watch."

It is a good watch, as it turns out—a 1940 Rolex with the
original nylon band. Its hands are painted with radium, and its
back is inscribed with my grandfather's name and RAF number. The band is in good shape, the restorer explained, probably
because my grandfather took it off after the war and never put
it on again. Whatever history the watch connected me to, my
grandfather wanted to forget all about it.

When I wear it now, the watch gives me a strange, unde-
served confidence. It's as if the watch were leading me (again,
like an amulet) with an almost tribal feeling, an intimate sense
of belonging to a numinous tradition that I could never articulate but that I would never be able to deny. It is the inarticulate
feeling of manliness, and at my father's funeral I needed that
manliness, even as an abandoned, nearly ruined accessory.

The hollow patriarchy is as much cultural as it is economic
or political; it exists in the clothes we wear, in advertising, in
slang, in novels and in the movies and in conversation. The rise
of equality implies doing away with difference. Feminism is a
humanism exactly because it refuses to limit the potential of
women and men based on gender. Anything boys can do, girls

can do. Anything girls can do, boys can do. And yet every bit
of culture, every inflection of voice, no matter how minor, remains gendered. The cut of a suit or the cinch of a belt, the line
of a melody or the arms of a sofa or the structure of a sentence
or the texture of a brush stroke—anything made by a human
being can be described in gendered terms. Culture calls out
for the duality, but any attempt to ascribe definite gendered
attributes to men or women falls apart like a soggy sandcastle.
The rise of equality between men and women should mean a
collapse of the concept of manliness and womanliness. It has
not. It will not. It leads instead to an order of masculinity and
femininity embraced and contained by permanent quotation
marks. It leads to straight camp.

* * *

I take it as given that the period of popular culture I lived
through, or rather through which my youth happened to pass,
between the late 1970s and the late 1990s, was the worst period
for popular culture of all time. I lived it. I can say it. Television
(*Dukes of Hazzard*, *Three's Company*, *Matlock*) was as stupid and
boring as it would ever be. Music was brittle (Depeche Mode),
empty (Madonna), self-righteous (U2), or suicidal (Nirvana).
The movies became opportunities to decorate cups at Burger
King. There are those in my generation—a noncommunal
community if one ever existed—who claim to love the material of our shared childhood; all I can say about their bizarre
thumb-sucking nostalgia is that they must long for their childhood with all the failure coiled in their high-expecting lives.

To be a pop culture critic in any period is to obsess over the quality of one's own shit. But the pop culture of the 1980s and 1990s was real shit. The most notable feature of the period—by no means a redeeming feature—was its flux and heave with absolute weirdness around men and women: weird hypermasculinity (the flexes of bodybuilders with their vermicular veins), weird unmasculinity (the rise of the conquering nerd), weird hyperfemininity (the impossible tits of Dolly Parton) against nascent androgyny (fourteen-year-old catwalk models). It was a mess, a tacky mess of a million absurd poses. Nancy Reagan sitting on the lap of Mr. T dressed as Santa. Arnold Schwarzenegger marrying a Kennedy. Cher riding the guns of the USS *Missouri*. It was super weird.

In the middle of all this weirdness I had only one beacon of clarity: *Free to Be You and Me*, the only cultural artifact of my childhood that addressed gender politics outright. The 1972 album release, which has sold in the vicinity of half a million copies, was followed by a bestselling book in 1974 and a television special that got massive ratings. I can still sing almost every song, recite almost every monologue. *Free to Be You and Me* has to be one of the most successful pieces of propaganda ever made. I'm not sure I've ever been truly close with anyone who wasn't raised on it. For me it defines prerational gender assumptions. The dialogue between two babies, played by Marlo Thomas and Mel Brooks, made a whole spiel out of shattering gender stereotypes. Alan Alda retelling the story of Atalanta as a woman who makes her own decisions about her future, an explanation of how advertising lies when it portrays smiling moms doing housework, why Dudley wants a doll: these are scenes from my childhood assumptions. Every time I deviate from the explicit political opinions of that album, a minor thrill of taboo violation goes through me. Part of its appeal is that it conjures up the innocence of presexual childhood and a world without the overwhelming consciousness of differentiation and diffusion. It remains my Utopia.

In my own life *Free to Be You and Me* was at the center, and the pop culture explosion of extreme gender dualities—Parton, Schwarzenegger—was at the periphery. The reverse was the case for the wider culture: there wrestling was the norm, equality was exotic. The culture that rises with the end of the gender wars is livid with the tension between the two sides: the humanistic rationalism of equality and the monstrosity of elaborated personae, a world in which boys and girls are the same and another world in which boys want to be Jake the Snake and girls want to be Malibu Barbie. A culture that dreams of gender equality also dreams of supermen and living dolls. The feeling of being a man or the feeling of being a woman shimmers on the skin, but the source of its potency is that it roots itself all the way down. It feels like the opposite of a choice. It feels as natural as anything human.

* * *

Gender difference is not one difference among others; it is the first to be noticed, the most prevalent, the most enduring. One group of social psychologists found that, of twenty different types of "natural distinctions," gender was by far the most significant. Sex is the first question asked about a newborn, even before health, and our tendency to make this distinction remains instinctive. It's been noticed in babies as young as three months. Adults can tell whether a person is a man or a woman from the way they walk in "as little as 2.7 seconds," according to psychophysical researchers. Insofar as human beings are capable of making distinctions at all, we distinguish between men and women. It is the fundamental mode of differentiation, which means that the way you feel about the differences between men and women doesn't solely reflect your feelings about men and women; it also reflects your feelings about difference itself.

Thirty years ago third-wave feminism took Simone de Beauvoir's famous dictum "One is not born, but rather becomes, a woman" as a starting point and began to question how we live gender rather than how we think about it. The legal gains, the economic gains, the intellectual gains had no cultural equivalent. Magazines and television and film commented elaborately on the feminist revolution; they failed almost completely to reflect it. This remains true: the standard forms of masculine and feminine beauty have remained remarkably static. Between Grace Kelly and Gwyneth Paltrow, or indeed between Cary Grant and George Clooney, there is a transfer from black and white to color and little else.

Until very recently, women's magazines* offered the same

---

*Actually Steve doesn't read many women's magazines, and I'm not sure he's right here. I recently picked up a copy of *Glamour* and found advice they have since the 1980s: how to look pretty, how to cook well, how to run an organized house, how to give blow-jobs. A lot of them now feature "how she does it" columns on career and family. This was a standard bromide of 1950s magazine profiles. Whenever the culture industry tries to be progressive, it's reliably a hilarious misstep. "We're going to show 'real women,' 'women with curves,'" who turn out to be size 6. Powerful women, on those startling and rare occasions when they appear, are throwbacks—Tina Fey on *30 Rock* is an updated version of Mary Tyler Moore—the powerful woman as outlier and misfit. Hollywood is supposedly a slave to the marketplace and left-wing politics. It certainly is excellent at throwing a vast self-congratulatory orgy whenever a minuscule milestone has been passed. But the truth is the culture industry is as hidebound as they come. Between 2009 and 2013 only 4.7 percent of feature films released by the six biggest Holly-wood studios were directed by women. Even more incredibly, only one female director in all those films directed two features. That's a single woman. Of the one hundred top-grossing films of 2013, 1.9 percent of the directors were female. It gets worse. Ninety-eight percent of films in the one hundred top-grossing films have more male than female characters. Of 4,506 speak-

---

almost every page had a feminist flavor. There was a photo essay on the women running the American presidential campaigns, a Q&A with the feminist comedian Tig Notaro, and a page on clothing that featured lionizing images of Ruth Bader Ginsburg. Reading it was uplifting, and I nearly signed up for a subscription.

ing parts, 29.2 percent were for women, 28 percent were female leads, and only 16 percent were in films that had gender
parity. The hack of Sony emails revealed that the pay gap between male and female Hollywood stars is substantial. Even
the biggest stars of the moment—Charlize Theron and Jennifer
Lawrence—make millions less than their male counterparts.*
Hollywood is far less welcoming to women than the Republican Party is.

Naomi Wolf's *The Beauty Myth* examined this landscape
with classic mid-1990s nuance and sophistication and took it
all as evidence of conspiracy. "We are in the midst of a violent
backlash against feminism that uses images of female beauty as
a political weapon against women's advancement," Wolf wrote.
"It is seeking right now to undo psychologically and covertly all
the good things that feminism did for women materially and
overtly." Not merely a stand-in for oppression, the representation
of women was the root of oppression itself. If "images of female
beauty" were the new weapons, magazines, television shows,
and movies were to be disarmed; pop culture took the place of
government and business as the enemy to be overcome, and the

---

*Study after study after study show that men ask for more money way
more often than women do. I've read all those studies, and I know it to
be true from my own experience. My male employees ask me for salary
increases two or three times more often than my female employees.
And yet, despite knowing all this, despite knowing that pay equity is a
real problem and that it is partly based on the female employee not
valuing her own work as much as men value theirs, I myself have only
ever asked for a raise once—and guess what? I got it.

way to overcome the forces of representation was by extensive, fulsome, elaborate critique, and occasionally protests outside Miss America pageants or the offices of *Seventeen* magazine or, in the United Kingdom, Tesco retailers that stacked lad mags.

The Beauty Myth was a strong polemic in the sense that it had the strength to reduce complex realities to a manageable figment. Its epigraph came from Virginia Woolf: "It is far more difficult to murder a phantom than a reality." An apt metaphor: the way you murder a phantom is by showing the world that it is a phantom. But in this case the phantom continued its haunting. Part of the problem was that *The Beauty Myth* could not bring itself to be prescriptive. Wolf argued for openness and selfishness, for intellectual consumerism: "Let's be shameless. Be greedy. Pursue pleasure. Avoid pain. Wear and touch and eat and drink what we feel like. Tolerate other women's choices." But what does that mean? Ultimately vacuous bromides about shamelessness and pleasure were placeholders, a means of negotiating future embarrassments: Loretta Lynn singing about the Pill in the frilliest of frilly dresses, and later Nicki Minaj showing off her ass as proof of power. In the absence of new ideals of femininity, the old ones flooded back in. But it was a convenient incoherence: you could work yourself into a lather over something as negligible as a new line of lipstick. You could take Beyoncé singing "Bootylicious" as feminist iconography. You could justify what you liked. You could condemn what you didn't.

Choice was the word that tolled like a bell over the morass of this lousy culture and its critics. The economic basis of women's liberation made no other kind of critique possible. Women have come up through the middle class, and choice has always been the banner under which the middle class marches. Thus the nature of the freedom, the brand of pride: "You have earned the money. You decide what to do with it." The economics of women's rise has been inherently individualistic.

Only tangentially does Wolf acknowledge that the market for the beauty myth is almost entirely female: men do not produce or consume *Vogue* or Katherine Heigl movies or *Martha Stewart Living*. Because Wolf ignores, or rather excuses as taught self-hatred, the fact that women have made the beauty myth themselves, the real mystery of the period eludes her: why women who collectively earned vastly more money and achieved remarkably more power and insisted to an unprecedented degree on their full humanity would buy cultural material on how to look pretty, how to cook a good meal, and how to give better blowjobs.

The feminism of choice is not inherently progressive; it is indifferent to but also transcends the content of women in culture. So long as women choose to do what they do, their choices are beyond judgment. They may choose to have sex with other women. They may choose not to have babies. They may choose to shave their heads. But also: They may choose to attend wet T-shirt contests. They may choose to stay home and cook for their husband. They may choose to wear a burka. Women choosing to do exactly what patriarchy has always told them to do cannot be questioned, their right to self-determination being an absolute value.

* * *

Choice feminism has no specific content, but that doesn't mean it's static; the old iconography remains but the meaning underlying it has shifted. In the magazines of the 1950s women learned how to cook soufflés; in the magazines of the 2010s too, women learn how to cook soufflés, but the motive of the readers and the writers has changed, and so everything has changed. A screen has been drawn between women and their objectification.

The act of citation has become the act of power. Models in the pages of *Vogue* may imitate porn stars without fear of being confused with the real thing because the gesture of citation demonstrates how removed they really are from the status of sexual utensil. Hipsters may dress like Emily Dickinson because the gesture of citation demonstrates how conscious they are of their own sleek modernity. Citation is fashion's will to power, and it is reflected on every level. For *Cosmo* magazine how to give a man the best orgasm of his life is the way to empowerment, and for the *Gentlewoman* it is creating idiosyncratic narratives out of clothing. The process is the same—empowerment through the projection of a chosen femininity—but the level of projection is much more distinct in the latter, and therefore more sophisticated, and therefore more powerful. The clarity and detail of the femininity in the *Gentlewoman* oozes money.

The tiny crack between image and identity may be nearly invisible, but it is the whole point of empowered cultural practice. "For the girl, erotic transcendence consists in making herself prey in order to make a catch," de Beauvoir wrote in *The Second Sex*. "She becomes an object; and she grasps herself as object; she is surprised to discover this new aspect of her being; it seems to her that she has been doubled; instead of coinciding exactly with her self, here she is existing *outside* of her self." That doubleness, the self-alienation, has gone nowhere, but it has transferred beyond the gaze of men and other women. Clothes are worn for the mirror, for the selfie. A young woman still becomes an object, but she becomes an object for herself. She becomes her own prey. She preys on her own identity. She only baits the clothes with her body.

Coco Chanel, the inventor of modern fashion, made herself into a luxury product for men. Tavi Gevinson, the creator and editor of *Rookie* magazine and the future of fashion, makes herself into a luxury product for herself. Chanel made herself fascinating; Gevinson finds the world fascinating. Chanel was a mistress; Gevinson is mistress of herself. Chanel once said, in desperate pride as much as in humiliation, "Those on whom legends are built *are* their legends." Chanel was a dark genius, a genius of the type the world shouldn't need. That is the labyrinthine mess of the self we call glamour. Gevinson has herself. She is building her own legend.

The insertion of a screen between women and their objectification means that women may choose to play at any femininity they like, so long as it remains clear they are choosing. As a man I envy this fluidity. The cultural wars of feminism have been nasty, but they have given women a vast trunk of costumes to put on, each with its own strength and weakness.

Radical lesbian. Wife and mother. Scholar. Prostitute. Quirky and independent *urbaniste*. CEO. One may be a woman in a hundred different ways at a hundred different moments. Christine Lagarde, head of the International Monetary Fund, an economic assassin, the woman who said of the Greeks during their economic crisis, "They should help themselves collectively by paying their tax," keeps a caricature of herself in fishnet stockings on the wall of her office. Why shouldn't she? Nobody believes she is brutalizing the world's bankers in a feminine way. The intellectual incoherence of third-wave feminism, so far from being weakness, has been a source of strength—an embrace of life's messiness, a willingness to ride on the surface of things. The ease of movements between the various registers of being is the contemporary form of grace.

In this mobility and grace men are thirty years behind women, if not fifty, if not a hundred. Feminism has articulated a dizzying variety of positive ways to be a woman.* Men remain obsessed mostly with how not to be a man.

* * *

My grandfather wore the watch while he was flattening German cities. He served as a rear gunner in a Lancaster bomber. Alone, in the dark, in silence, in a cold that sometimes

---

*Yes, providing you look nice. Lagarde is a trim, attractive sixty-year-old woman with great scarves and an expensive haircut. Feminism has made many things possible for women, but not for women who are fat, ugly, or old. Show me a powerful female Chris Christie or Rob Ford.

dipped to 15 below, he waited behind the infamously weak guns of the Lancaster for German fighters to cruise up behind him into shooting range. The average survival rate for an RAF rear-gunner was four missions. My grandfather flew fifty. (Incidentally he did not receive any extraordinary medals for this service; seventy years ago such actions were not considered worthy of commendation.)

In the sunny summers in New Brunswick I slept on a cot in a room whose walls were lined with guns. My grandfather had worked at a Canadian Pacific tin shop, and some of the guns he had built himself. His medals too were in that room, but forgotten, hidden under a collection of board games in the closet, where I would rustle around on rainy days. A treasure eventually emerged from my digging: my grandfather's war diary. A real-life horror story. A nightmare that was lived. He would pass out from fear and wake up after landing, covered in vomit. He wrote with painful blankness about making friends who died a week later and the loneliness of being a farm boy in London during the Blitz. His main theme was longing for "Bertie," my grandmother Roberta. No doubt my preoccupation with stories and their power dates from this scene: I am lying in the faint smell of mothballs and rain, restless, perusing the records of a grand passion, a grand agony, while on the ground floor, impossibly, my smiling, slightly walleyed grandfather sits mildly stoned on rum and pineapple juice, watching whatever happens to be on television, and my grandmother tidies the kitchen. I would walk down to them later, and they would rouse into their performances of themselves, while I knew the impossible currents of their subterranean lives and said nothing. I still write my best stuff lying in bed.

My grandfather's watch is an antique object of masculinity, a memento of the strong and silent type that the Second World War produced in masses, the men who returned from the war against evil and never spoke about it. My grandfather did his duty and didn't make a big deal of it. That's still what we mean when we say "Act like a man." We don't mean "Give a performance of manliness"; we mean "Stop performing." Masculinity has an anti-aesthetic aesthetic at its core. Straight men have lived with this paradox since the Second World War: to perform manliness is to be unmanly. It is a paradox that lives in silence and a peculiar species of sadness and a willful forgetfulness about the biological and emotional realities of men. It lives in self-hatred too and empty arrogance and a host of tortured and corrupt poses.

Masculinity today has become practically synonymous with degradation. Conjure up the image of a young man, and you automatically picture a loser. He lives in his parents' basement, alternating video games and porn, presumably underemployed from either inclination or bad luck. Naturally he never reads; that's for pussies. He eats burgers wrapped in pizzas or donut egg sandwiches or anything covered in bacon. He hangs out with his childhood friends doing childish things unless absolutely forced to do otherwise. This man-boy, basically the stock male character of all contemporary comedies, converts somewhere in his thirties into the reluctant dad, the guy who really wants to be drinking beer rather than talking with his wife or driving his kids around. Why women would fall in love with these boys or the men they half-turn-into is a mystery: lack of other options, or the attractions of condescension?

The contemporary American male retreats whenever possible. The "man cave" is a perfect articulation of the situation men find themselves in; they can recover their manliness only in hiding, in a physical retreat that is simultaneously a retreat in time. The contemporary man cave is for the contemporary caveman. The figure of the man who is proud of his masculinity, who revels in it, is almost inevitably the douchebag. He struts through the world, daring it to despise his crudity. The douchebag has no taste and no values and no discipline. He calls himself a jackass. He's proud to be in an entourage, a professional hanger-on. He possesses all the iconography of traditional male power and wants to own stupidly expensive markers of that power. The expense is primarily what matters. The douchebag does not drive a Jaguar E-type. He drives a Hummer. Or, even better, an ironically polluting diesel-spewing tractor-trailer.

*   *   *

The despicable shibboleth of the new hypermasculinity is the word *bro*. After *The Fast and the Furious* and *How I Met Your Mother* and *Breaking Bad*, if a show contains more than one male character under the age of fifty, they will, at some point, call each other by that name. Online, where cliché is rechristened as meme, *bro* is a natural epithet: "Come at me, bro," or "Don't tase me, bro." Among writers who are trying to be funny the word has morphed into a series of fused words, comic portmanteaus (portmanbros, if you insist), which have coagulated into a full-on brocabulary: *brogrammers*, for young male computer programmers; *brostep*, for a white male version of dubstep; *curlbros*, for bros who spend too much time on their biceps. Anything that men do in groups, any activity whatsoever, they do as bros.

Subject to intense semantic distortion and fluctuation, the word *bro* is slippery, but one feature of its use and abuse remains constant: the underlying contempt for male friendship it implies. No less an authority than the *Oxford English Dictionary* has traced the history of the word only to be flummoxed by the range of its contemporary usage. In the 1970s the word shifted from being a short form of *brother* to being an epithet used among African Americans. At the same time, among surfers the word *brah* drifted across from Hawaii. *Bro* has since become almost exclusively a term of usage among white men. The *OED* identifies one of its stranger properties: "a certain element of metonymy: by being the sort of person who says 'bro,' a person becomes a bro." The word is fluid, almost untranslatable into its own language, and much like the word *hipster* it has become embroiled in its own opposition, at least among people who care about what *bro* might or might not mean. The word has "a level of nuance that a conventional dictionary entry is ill-suited to describe: the semantic boundaries are subjective and in constant flux."

One major function of the word is to give women with an Ivy League education a chance to mock lower-class men. *Jezebel* posted a "Field Guide to Bros" in 2014. The critique encompassed dress as varied as "salmon colored shorts," "plaid shirts," and "ill-fitting business casual" and activities as distinct as "reading the *New Yorker* on the train" and "attending church services." The *Jezebel* bro would include professors of semiotics and construction workers, black men and white men, the intelligent and the lunkheaded, the fey and the macho. *Bro*, in their reading, is indistinguishable from *young middle-class American male*, and their use of the term is a signifier of their cool comic-edged misandry, sort of the verbal equivalent of wearing a T-shirt that says "I bathe in male tears."

The first portmanbro the *OED* could find was from a surfing magazine. *Bromance* is the ideal as well as the original portmanbro. Men who love each other are either clandestine homosexuals or homophobes or probably both. The polyvalence of the term allows for its audience to pick which insult it prefers. All forms of male community are connected with one another: fraternities with anime fan gatherings, soldiers with men who hang around in cafés talking about their creative writing courses, corporate board members and skateboarders. All are men in groups. All are bros. The actual content of the contempt is irrelevant, so long as it is there.

In popular culture the friendships between women are the source and the choicest fruit of their maturity. In the final scene of Noah Baumbach's 2012 film *Frances Ha*, Frances glimpses her oldest friend across a crowded room. "Who are you making eyes at?" somebody asks. "That's Sophie. She's my best friend." And we know that theirs was the film's true love story all along. Insofar as any given television show is about women, it's about friendship—*Sex and the City*, *Girls*, *Broad City*, and

so on. Male friendship on any given sitcom, or in any Judd
Apatow movie, is a retreat into thoughtlessness, crudity. *The
Big Lebowski* hilariously painted male friendship as an extended
and colossal fuckup. The *Hangover* movies turned it into a series of epic degradations—involving Mike Tyson and a tiger in
Las Vegas, ladyboys in Bangkok, and waking up in a bathroom
with breast implants. But the standard buddy movie of the moment, a movie like *22 Jump Street*, is defined by a single word:
dumb. That's why the greatest buddy movie of them all is *Dumb
and Dumber*. Men get together onscreen to be idiots with one
another. To mature as a female person is to mature into female
friendships. To mature as a male person is to mature out of
male friendships.

It should come as no surprise, then, that the culture that
has given rise to the word *bro* is a culture in which male friendship is in crisis. The transition from boyhood to manhood is a
journey into isolation. Becoming a man means leaving behind
your family and your friends, striking out on your own. And
therefore growing up means shedding connections. Male suicide rates correlate precisely to the loss of their friendships. At
age nine suicide rates are the same for girls and boys. Between
ten and fourteen, boys are twice as likely to kill themselves. Between fifteen and nineteen, they are four times as likely. From
twenty to twenty-four, five times.

Masculine maturity is inherently a lonely thing to possess.
That's why maturity and despair go together for men. The
splendid isolation of masculinity has emerged from so much
iconography—the cowboy, the astronaut, the gangster—that

almost every hero in the past fifty years has been a figure of loneliness. Current pop culture is even more extreme: it doesn't merely celebrate the lonely man; it despises men in groups. That contempt runs counter to male biology. Men, every iota as much as women, are social creatures who live in a permanent state of interdependence and require connection for basic happiness. In periods of vulnerability the male suicide rate spikes. Unemployed men kill themselves twice as often as employed men. (There's no difference in the rates for employed and unemployed women.) After divorce a man is ten times as likely to commit suicide as a woman. Men over eighty-five kill themselves thirteen times more often than women over eighty-five.

Suicide has become the leading cause of death by injury in America, surpassing car accidents. According to the Centers for Disease Control and Prevention, in 2010, the most recent year for which data are available, there were 38,364 suicides and 33,687 deaths by car accident. And the major reason for that change is a cohort shift. The group that has shown the highest increase in suicide rates is middle-aged men, for whom the number of suicides has risen by a horrifying 28.4 percent in a mere decade; among that group the rate for men in their fifties has risen nearly 50 percent since 1999.

The reasons for this rise are speculative. The increased availability of prescription drugs may play some role, since poisoning has become a common method of suicide. There have never been more guns in America, and gun ownership correlates to an increase in suicide. There has also been the brutality of the recession and the new reality of people in middle age taking care of elderly parents while they're also taking care of young children. Economic pressures are the most compelling reason; for example, after the 2008 crash the number of suicides increased globally by 3.3 percent. The more substantial, and more complicated and disturbing answer is cultural. Suicide is not connected to religious values or traditional family structure. It is directly related to loneliness, to social isolation. And not only are American men more likely to be lonely, but they are also more likely to deny their loneliness.

Who needs research to understand the difference? Look at the women around you—your mother, your sister, your wife, or your girlfriend. How many people can they call when they have a bad day? And the men?

*   *   *

Without friendships life simply isn't worth much. Friendship is essential not just to a personal sense of well-being but to society. In *The Nicomachean Ethics* Aristotle prizes it more than justice: "When men are friends, they have no need of justice, while when they are just they need friendship as well, and the truest form of justice is thought to be a friendly quality." Note that Aristotle says "friendship," not "bromance."

Bro is a light word encumbered by shadow. It is a joke aglow in an aura of suffering. Both the men who use it as a password for a community of idiots and the outsiders who use it as a cipher for contempt mean to imply the darkness and the suffering as much as the lightness and the joking. They respect fundamentally only the lonely man, the man who is by himself.

They betray, by that respect, the deep traditionalism of their vision of masculinity, the man who needs no other.

That traditional masculinity must wither and die unless we insist that men themselves wither and die. The sophistication of adult male friendship is essential to being a fully formed person. Men need friendships the way they need oxygen, in blood and bone. The current contempt cannot last because the lesson for men is obvious: Keep your bros. Just don't call them that.

*   *   *

How did manhood become synonymous with crudity? *The Beauty Myth* blamed a vague patriarchy for the state of femininity in mass culture. It would be stupid to repeat that mistake when it comes to the decrepitude of masculinity. Men have themselves constructed the palace of shit they inhabit.

A recent series of studies from UC Berkeley tested what sociologists call "the masculine overcompensation thesis," the theory that when men feel their masculinity is threatened, they respond by exaggerating their masculine traits. The researchers found that when men were given feedback that they were feminine, they tended to increase their support for war, homophobia, male dominance, and "purchasing an SUV." Women do not respond this way. If you give women feedback that they are masculine, they don't suddenly want to buy a pink Prius. Overcompensation always tends to devolve into its crudest traits. Globally we are living in the midst of macho taken to the point of a joke—most obviously in the glistening prick who was Silvio Berlusconi. But maybe most chillingly in the case of Vladimir Putin, he who wrestles with tigers, who dives for amphorae in the Black Sea, the expressionless judo master who brings a dog on state visits with Angela Merkel because he knows she hates them, the frightened tyrant overseeing a failed state shellacked in virility. Donald Trump, as a political phenomenon, is the purest possible expression of masculine overcompensation in the history of the Republic.

But in America you can see the history of masculine over-compensation, with its willful, intentional drive to crudity, most clearly in the novelists. The iconic American male writers of the postwar period—especially the great ones—responded to the rise of women with fear and puff-chested emptiness. When Norman Mailer wrote "The sniffs I get from the ink of the women are always fey, old-hat, Quaintsy Goysy, tiny, too dykily psychotic, crippled, creepish, fashionable, frigid, outer-Baroque, *maqueillé* in mannequin's whimsy, or else bright and stillborn," he was re-acting to the fact that there had emerged dozens of female writers better than he: Germaine Greer, Margaret Atwood, Toni Morrison. Only a threatened man would utter such nonsense.

Philip Roth, the greatest male novelist of his generation, turned himself into a well-established brand of forgiven misogyny. When Portnoy timidly offers to buy a shiksa a drink, she sneers. When he violently claims he wants to eat her pussy, she approves: "We went to her apartment, where she took off her clothes and said, 'Go ahead.'" This is an amazingly common fantasy: that by being an asshole, you score. The strategy might even work, but here's the thing: even when it does, you're still an asshole.

Roth is a great writer, but all his books are an angry reaction. Like all inherently angry men, what he craves is pity. He longs desperately to fit himself into the new status of victimology that emerged out of the 1960s. All of Roth's great late novels contain that inversion. Established men, of the most dominant sort in the most traditional positions of power, turn out to be victims. So *American Pastoral* works this way: the Swede is a successful factory owner—rich, white, privileged—but the real story is he's the one being fucked over. In the most welcoming country and period in the history of the Jewish people, Roth wrote *The Plot Against America*, an imagined counterhistory in which America is a great anti-Semitic power. In *The Human Stain* Coleman Silk is a white classics professor—and so not entitled to pity—but then it turns out, magically, that he's black, and so entitled to pity. Roth has proven to be a devoted, clandestine apprentice of the identity politics he claims to revile.

Postfeminist machismo has essentially dissolved in the absurdity of its own premises. It was never entirely credible because it was so obviously on the losing side. Roth is, deservedly, one of the most widely admired writers in America, but no one wants to write like him. He has no imitators; he influences no one. The sad young literary men adore him, rally to his defense whenever he's attacked, but don't kid yourself: at their desks they're all trying to be Alice Munro. He wrote books that sting. They write books that soothe.*

---

*Alice Munro stories sting too. They can be totally devastating, no?

Mailer and Roth, and John Updike too, tried on the recognizable self-loathing braggadocio of teenage boys well into their seventies, terrified of the fact of their body and of the seemingly oceanic negotiations required for intimacy. The septuagenarians and the teenage boys aren't wrong to be afraid; equality is terrifying. You put your soul at risk. And so it's much easier to pose as if you'd cheerfully trade your soul for a little anal. But this crude masculinity won't do for too much longer. It pretends to be "men as they really are," but it's obviously as much a mask as anything else. And only the desperate would wear such a stupid, self-loathing mask for long.

Men are obviously at the end of something, possibly of many things, but each ending is also a beginning. You won't find the hope in books or even on screen, but there's a glimmer in the clothes men wear on the street. In his *Treatise on Elegant Living*, Balzac wrote a series of maxims for men of style. Number 40 is "Clothing is how society expresses itself." Men's clothing of the moment is an expression of a deep contradiction: the weak act hard and the hard act weak. At a rib festival in a poor suburb of my city, where mostly working-class families consumed big slabs of slow-cooked meat on plastic benches with the music of a Neil Diamond cover band drifting overhead, the vast majority of men, particularly the young men, looked "hard," with bicep-baring shirts, chunky jewelry, and extensive arrays of tattoos. Because they had no money, they wore their money. Because they had no power, they displayed power. The following week I happened to be at a bris in the very choicest neighborhood of the city. A bris with valet parking. There the softness of the clothes was reminiscent of a weekend at the cottage, the shirts hanging out, the shorts frayed, everyone in sandals, the vague hint of antique English soap and sand from exclusive beaches. There were people worth hundreds of millions of dollars in that room. Wearing rags showed how invulnerable they were.

Strength means weakness and weakness means strength. The man in the salmon-colored shirt fires the man in overalls. A face covered with Nazi tattoos is the face of a man as powerless as it is possible to be. Mark Zuckerberg, emanating gentle geekiness, projects his billions. Snoop Dogg changed his name to Snoop Lion; it was a sign that his gangster life—which played so weak by acting so hard—was ending, and true self-determination was emerging. When Jay Z rapped about "Big Pimpin'" he was expressing how powerless he was as a young black man. Now he appears on the subway talking politely to nice Jewish ladies who don't recognize him. That's power. That's a man who knows what he's about.

Masculine sensibility has turned into a game of leveling. Strength can mean weakness, which can again mean strength. Michael Cera plays an asshole to prove that he's a nice guy who was raised in a secure middle-class family. Kanye West insults other singers, which proves he's vulnerable, which demonstrates that he has overcome hardships. The choice that emerged for women, the screen drawn between the self and its objectification, is beginning, just beginning, to intrude into the lives of men.

*   *   *

Masculinity and femininity, in terms of their cultural expressions, dwell in an infinitely varying, endlessly expanding series of citations, for men and women both. For women, these citations are a means of escape and retrenchment. For men citations are a way of negotiating the end of patriarchal norms. In both cases, straight sexuality is becoming theatrical, and the farther we go the more extreme that theatricality grows. The most popular of popular culture exemplifies gender performativity: For women, the Kardashians, the "real" housewives, Martha Stewart, and a hundred domestic goddesses perform elaborate parodies of feminine traits, taken seriously and comically at once. For men, *The Deadliest Catch*, *Ice Road Warriors*, and *Duck Dynasty* show tough guys wrestling with the forces of nature for the amusement of deskbound data analysts. They show bearded men doing ludicrously "manly" things, with the manliness firmly kept in quotation marks. Donald Trump, as a pop culture figure, is basically walking "manliness." In the welter of back and forth, in the froth of the display, straight camp is emerging. Straight camp defines the current cultural reality of masculinity and femininity.

Susan Sontag defined *camp* in the 1960s as an aspect of gay sensibility, a self-conscious performance of a clandestine sexual identity. Camp is a theatricality of desire. "Camp sees everything in quotation marks. It's not a lamp, but a 'lamp'; not a woman, but a 'woman.' To perceive Camp in objects and persons is to understand Being-as-Playing-a-Role. It is the farthest extension, in sensibility, of the metaphor of life as theater." Gay speech was coded speech. Gay desire was coded desire, a flight

from its own secrecy and shame, ultimately a flight from acknowledgment of its own existence. And through the metaphor
of life as theater, camp converted the variety of sexual desire
into elaborate play in a mirrored cave.

Through a vast organization effort and personal struggle,
gay people in Western democracies have shrugged off the need
for camp. They have embedded their self-worth in the public
institutions that give societal solidity to straight sexuality. They
decided to stop hiding in theatricality. They altered the meaning
of gayness in the process. The gay men I grew up around, went
to school with, and worked with lived this change. Many had
come from small towns. Many had been abandoned by their
families. They had to find work, support themselves, educate
themselves. Then a bunch of their friends died while they were
still in their midtwenties. When the bastards spat at them,
they organized. I compare these habits of life with those of my
straight male friends, in basements, in clouds of puff, dealing
with the fallout of one failure after another as lazily as possible.
The gay man used to be the sissy, the nancy-boy. Now the gay
man possesses the traditional virtues of a soldier, a husband,
the antithesis of camp. Meanwhile straightness has become a
big act.

Neil Patrick Harris represents the switch perfectly. When
he plays straight characters, like Barney in *How I Met Your
Mother* or "Neil Poon Hound" in the Harold and Kumar
movies, he plays them camped to the hilt, with an endless
surface of suits, strippers, motivational posters, hookers, and
drugs. Instead of morality he has the Brocode, something

closer to a code of etiquette for roving animals than an ethical system. Harris understands, perhaps better than any straight actor, how brittle hypermasculinity is. When Barney shatters, he shatters completely. As a person, or the approximation of personhood provided by celebrity, Harris has become an icon of the new gay normalcy, with the solid partner, the kids, even a separate room in his house for his favorite hobby (magic), and the easy confidence that comes from not taking yourself too seriously. As a celebrity gay man, he's practically too boring for a profile. On screen, as a straight guy, he's a freak in a perpetual identity crisis.

The quotation marks have shifted from gay to straight people. They're disconcerting at first, but also liberating. It is possible, for instance, to look like a lumberjack and be a stay-at-home dad, and to find no contradiction in that sensibility. It is possible to try having sex with a man without considering yourself gay. It is possible to like manicures and be a gangster. Masculinity and femininity are growing lighter, more fluid than ever before. Retreat and overcompensation are increasingly recognizable as signs of failure. The straight man as willful loser, the straight man as empty bastard, the douchebag, will go. Male and female sensibility will have to develop simply because the historical reality is developing. And we will have to decide what we want to keep from the past and what we want to throw away. What does a masculine style mean? What does a feminine style mean? Will it be closer to *Free to Be You and Me* or World Wrestling Entertainment? Or both? The two run parallel to one other: the single dream of equality and the many dreams of theatrical sexual style.

Straight camp means that you have a choice in how to be a man or a woman. It also means you must choose. The corollary of Balzac's Maxim 40 is Balzac's Maxim 41: "Negligence of clothing is moral suicide." The world of play can be delightful, but no one is exempted anymore. The dance may be joyful or sorrowful. But you must dance.

* * *

I choose to wear my grandfather's watch. It is a style that I put on. Its most powerful effect is that it liberates me from the sense of having a style. There are more important problems than the petty concerns you call your "worries," it says. You do not have to fly over German cities, bombing them to ensure the survival of democracy.

My father also flew for his country. In his twenties, though, midway through his training, he decided that he couldn't in all conscience bomb people. What honor could there be in flying thirty thousand feet in the air and ending the lives of tens of thousands of people indiscriminately? After he'd had many discussions with friends and then even more discussions with his superiors, the bureaucracy moved him over to a desk job involving the nascent, eccentric field of computing, on which basis he built another career.

Neither my grandfather nor my father ever spoke to me about life in the military. Their silence was similar, though their actions were distinct. One bombed; the other did not. Both had to make significant personal sacrifices in that act. This is what the watch makes me feel. It connects me to the world of men who lived with honor.

The nature and meaning of honor, the nature and meaning of what it meant to be a valuable man, changed and keeps changing. As I write this, the U.S. Army is integrating its forces. Women have taken command over six Virginia-class nuclear submarines. Does any sane person doubt that they'll do as good a job as men did? Seventy years from now some granddaughter will be restoring her grandmother's watch. Perhaps the Iraq war will be the last to fill America with a backwash of devastated young men; next time it will be devastated people. And the meaning of honor will shift once again.

Nevertheless I wear my grandfather's watch. It reminds me that honor still matters, despite the vagaries of the past seventy years. The value of honor may be confused and muddy and all play. But men without honor aren't worth anything, still.

The watch has survived when maybe it shouldn't have. It's kind of a pain in the ass. I have to wind it every morning. But somehow it keeps working.

FOUR

—

The Pornography Paradox

W HEN I was around twelve I caught a glimpse of a page ripped from a soft-core porn magazine in the trunk of my soccer coach's hatchback. I can still recall the image precisely, every detail: a woman standing on a ladder, a thong lowered to the midpoint of her thighs, in soft focus, with an angular haircut (possibly, now that I consider it, a wig), tossing behind her an over-the-shoulder gaze. A scene from a store catalogue, though more improbable and more naked. According to the cliché, pictures sear themselves into memory, and in this case the cliché is the only accurate description—a burning, an ineradicable mark. The power of the image of a naked lady then was due to its rarity. Today, nearly every time I search for a television show on my MacBook I see naked gyrating asses in the banner ads for chat rooms or live cams or escort services, and my son sometimes sees such images when he's beside me as I search. I barely notice them, partly because I'm no longer twelve and partly because they're so common. I suppose I should avoid them somehow, but the truth is that the naked gyrating asses are part of the background to my life, digital wallpaper in the pornified culture we inhabit.

I've lived the whole history of online pornography as it has darkly dawned over our intimate lives. In a world of cultural fragmentation, when even the most popular television shows and movies are seen only by niches of the population, Internet pornography is the one product that every man—every single man you meet—has encountered. Osama bin Laden, not only a Muslim extremist opposed to all forms of representation but a man with four wives, had his stash the same as everyone else—a "fairly extensive" stash, at least according to the SEALs, and who knows what they consider extensive. Every fourteen-year-old boy with an Internet connection has seen a woman anally penetrated with a baseball bat. YouPorn, one of maybe a dozen equally popular free porn sites, is six times bigger than Hulu; Xvideos, with 4.4 billion unique visitors a month—three times the size of CNN or ESPN—streams fifty gigabytes *per second*. When Pornhub released its data in 2013, it averaged 1.68 million views per hour. The only competitors for porn in terms of views are the Facebooks of the world, even though the vast majority of users come from only one gender. British prime minister David Cameron—a man who may or may not have fucked a dead pig, according to people who knew him in college—described pornography as "polluting the Internet." But pornography is too big to be pollution; it is a significant proportion of the Internet, and therefore a significant proportion of consciousness.

* * *

Panic has followed the porn surge. Male masturbation, far from being accepted with a lighthearted shrug as it once was, has become a political issue. Several countries, notably Iceland and Britain, have taken legislative steps to restrict online pornography. In Britain the issue achieved a rare cross-party consensus: an antiporn law requiring that Internet service providers include a porn filter on all streaming networks was passed by the Conservative government in July 2013 with the enthusiastic support of Labour. "I want to talk about the internet, the impact it is having on the innocence of our children, how online pornography is corroding childhood," Cameron said in announcing the law. "And how in the darkest corners of the internet, there are things going on that are a direct danger to our children, and that must be stamped out." Masturbation has become a source of mysterious abjection. What is all this porn doing to us? What is technological change doing to our most intimate lives?

No previous period in history has offered the brute exposure to sex that we take for granted. Never mind naked asses, how many images of vaginas have I seen in my lifetime? I couldn't possibly answer that question accurately, but I wouldn't be surprised if it were several thousand.* And I came

---

*Holy crap! Seriously? I've seen about a hundred and in the most conventional places: the copy of *Our Bodies, Ourselves* I owned in high school, my childhood friend's *Joy of Sex, Kama Sutra* postcards, stuff

to Internet pornography relatively late in my life, in my thirties. If I had been a teenager with a high-speed Internet connection, I imagine I would have see many tens of thousands more. That's more images of vaginas than all of my ancestors, collectively, could have dreamed of seeing.

Of the many differences between art and pornography, not the least significant is that pornography provides you with information. John Ruskin, the art critic who, among other intellectual achievements, defined the initial reception of Pre-Raphaelite painting, a man who studied nudes his whole life, famously couldn't manage to have sex with his wife on their wedding night. "It may be thought strange that I could abstain from a woman who to most people was so attractive," he declared during the annulment proceedings, in perhaps the least chivalrous public statement of all time. "But though her face was beautiful, her person was not formed to excite passion. On the contrary, there were certain circumstances in her person which completely checked it." His biographers have interpreted ."certain circumstances" to mean pubic hair. None of the statues he had studied possessed any.

Whatever the reason for Ruskin's ignorance, some aspect of a real woman would not gel with the ideals contained in his

---

on art gallery walls, and bits from avant-garde French cinema. As for penises, it's not how they look, it's what they do that matters. Many women love porn, but I find just about anything more interesting. Sex for me has nothing to do with voyeurism and everything to do with participation.

love of art. Pornography, like art, is a distorted fantasyland, but it is an instructional one. A young pornography viewer might be surprised by the presence of pubic hair in a real woman but only because it's so out of fashion at the moment. Pubic hair is now a way of carbon-dating pornography: the full bushes of the candlelit 1970s; the tense landing strips of the 1980s, surreptitiously mimicking thick lines of cocaine; the depilated present, with no obscurity whatsoever to the genital specimens. "Raised by porn" is an epithet used to describe an emotionless and clichéd lover who is sexually demanding and degrading. But those who are raised by porn know the physiology. No one needs to wonder what a blowjob is anymore; a million examples are a click away. The sexual manuals of the past are mostly hilarious in their triteness. They once considered acts currently performed in married couples' bedrooms several times a week to be the depths of illicit carnal knowledge.*

---

*At the same time that the market for pornography was expanding, there was a serious investment in sexual education and health—largely spearheaded by feminists. I don't think the power of this massive program of education should be underrated. When I was a teenager I listened to a popular Canadian radio call-in show hosted by a straight-talking nurse named Sue Johanson. I'd listen to it before falling asleep, on headphones attached to a bright yellow Sony Walkman, learning about menstruation, ovulation, masturbation, contraception, conception, lubrication, oral sex. I knew that having agency over my body meant understanding its mechanics. And I was lucky enough to have access to Johanson's show. Women in less permissive cultures are denied something life-alteringly big when they are denied access to sexual education.

Pornography, strictly as a visual medium, is the dark underside of enlightened sexual education. Not only do we see more sex than ever before but we think about sex more and we know more about sex. Any teenager who attends a high school that is not deliberately retrograde has seen a cross-section of an inserted erect penis or a molded plastic cast of labia minora nestled in labia majora, for some reason always in butcher's colors. Sexual exposure removes ignorance, removes mystery, removes danger. At the academic level sexuality has been researched to the point of blasé indifference. Flipping through the *Archives of Sexual Research* provokes serene boredom. I see there's a case study of a young man who suffers from eproctophilia, sexual attraction to the smell of farts. Well, why not? Whatever gets you through the night.

*   *   *

Massive sexual exposure is an inevitable result of two separate, though related sexual revolutions, both brought on by technological change. The Pill separated sexuality from procreation, and the computer screen has separated sexuality from the flesh. Both have opened vast new realms of sexual choice and openness, the climate necessary for the flourishing of pornography.

My wife's grandmother, Bubbe Helen, born in 1920, once told me that the ability to try each other out for a while before marriage was the best thing that happened to men and women in the twentieth century. I think she has to be right. We do not have to sleep with people for the rest of our lives because our parents think it's a good idea. We don't have to sleep with people for the rest of our lives because we guessed wrong. Sexuality has taken on the properties of cheerful consumerism: Go out and find whatever you like, as long as it's in your price range. Sexual consumerism, like any kind of consumerism, expands constantly the range and nature of the choices available. Viagra and the female equivalent, which is shortly to appear on the market, have made lust itself a calculation. Technology has expanded the options exponentially.

Pornography remains the model for the vast spectrum of choices the Internet can offer people. Don't like that ass? Swipe screen. That skin a bit too freckled? Swipe again. That convenience, that facility is being translated into every aspect of sexuality and human relationships. All problems of sex and dating are finding digital solutions. Ranges of lovers can be culled by algorithm or by curation: Want someone nearby to have sex with? There's Grindr or Tinder, to taste. Want to find out if a new guy is worth your time? There's Lulu. Couples' apps like Kahnoodle can gamify your relationship if you want a gamified relationship. And we are only at the beginning. No doubt every relationship problem we can identify—from how to meet people you wouldn't ordinarily meet to how to communicate sexual desires you can't articulate to yourself and how to live with other people's secrets—will eventually find a proposed technological solution. And why not? Why shouldn't we have relationship algorithms? The search for intimacy has to begin somewhere. Why not algorithms? The other way is booze.

The emphasis on personal choice in our sex lives has an intellectual and political corollary: the idea of "consenting adults." In a world of overwhelming sexual variety, consent becomes elevated to a sacred principle; it underlies the newly emerging consensus around sex, a consensus that is legal as well as social. All sexuality will eventually be judged on the basis of whether it is between consenting adults. In the 1960s pedophilia and homosexuality were both considered sexual diseases. Now homosexuality is an acceptable act because it is between consenting adults, while pedophilia, because it is a violation of consent, is a monstrous evil. Throughout history, pedophilia has frequently been acceptable when sexual acts between grown men were not. Even as recently as a decade ago pedophilia was punished by prison sentences of as little as two or three years. In 2012 Jerry Sandusky—the child molesting assistant coach at Penn State— was sentenced to sixty years.

As a complete system for comprehending human desire, consent is as arbitrary a basis as any other sexual morality. Adultery becomes purely a matter of the violated contract of marriage, not a social crime. Bestiality remains criminal, however; it is more socially acceptable to kill a pig than to fuck one because a pig cannot offer sexual consent. The major sexual conundrums of our time are questions of muddled consent. In Germany, for instance, the legalization of prostitution hinges on the question of whether prostitutes constitute "consenting adults" and on what terms their consent is granted. The conflict between pro- and antiprostitution activists is between two visions of the act itself: one in which prostitutes are independent contractors who willingly sell the labor of their bodies and another in which prostitutes are sexual slaves. Almost nobody, except outdated moralists like the Catholic Church, believes that the act itself—exchanging sex for money—is inherently wrong. (There are others who ask whether money is merely another species of compulsion.) Polygamy is stigmatized because of the abuse widely reported in poly marriages, but theoretically who can object to an arrangement undertaken between multiple rational and consenting adults? No one minds that Tilda Swinton is living with an old guy and a young guy. That's her choice. The question of surrogate pregnancy is problematic exactly because it involves a seemingly irresolvable contest between two competing claims to control—the genetic material in the womb and the woman whose womb it has filled. Contemporary sexuality is a subset of contract law.

In all of these difficult new problems, progressive forces—particularly the joint powers of feminism and gay rights—may seem like crusaders for openness and tolerance. They are in fact promoters of a new morality based on the principle of consent. I share this morality, I should add. It is an enlightened humanistic morality, based on personal dignity and the sanctity of rational choice. But the triumph of consent as a guiding principle to distinguish good and bad sexuality has a host of unintended consequences, which we live through in our bodies. Pornography is only the subterranean example.

* * *

The most obvious consequence of the rise of choice-centered, consent-based morality, and it has to be said the most important, is that sex has become much healthier, much less shameful, and, if not much better, a great deal less tortured.

Not that you would believe it from reading most reporting on the subject. The explosion of wild and dangerous promiscuity is a staple of the think-piece. *Vanity Fair* ran an article in October 2012 on the impact of porn and social media on teenagers. Because of porn, the author claimed, young women feel pressured to post explicit images online, to behave like actresses in porn films. "When you have sex with a guy, they want it to be like a porno," a nineteen-year-old girl said. "They want anal and oral right away." Such articles may make for unsettling reading, but they are based almost exclusively on anecdotal evidence. The empirical evidence should comfort the hearts of the most conservative of old-timers. In a world overwhelmed by porn, the U.S. teenage pregnancy rate is declining precipitously. In 2011 the Centers for Disease Control and Prevention reported that, for the first time, teenagers who had had sex were in the minority. Teenagers wait longer to have sex, and for the right reasons: either because it is "against their religion or morals" or because "they had not yet found the right person." They may talk about ten-dollar blowjobs in their school bathroom or enforced orgies as initiation for the cool kids, but the best evidence we have suggests a trend the other way. The Internet Age, for teenagers, is an age of relative prudery.

Once people start having sex, however, they really have sex. It is great that men and women have time to try each other out, as Bubbe Helen said. The 2010 National Survey of Sexual Health and Behavior from Indiana University showed how thoroughly they are doing so. As recently as 1992 oral sex was considered "surprisingly ubiquitous." By their late twenties over 90 percent of women have performed fellatio, 50 percent in the past month. The same goes for men and cunnilingus. Experimenting with homosexuality and straight anal sex are on the rise too. In 1992, 16 percent of women between eighteen and twenty-four said they'd tried anal sex; in 2015 the rate was 40 percent for women between the ages of twenty and twenty-four.

So, on the one hand, young men and women are waiting longer to have sex. They are having sex for better reasons. When they do have sex, they have sex with less shame and are more open to all avenues of pleasure. What has happened to us, in a phrase, is that we have become sensible about sex. We have made sex rational. We should celebrate.

*   *   *

The horrors of pornography have emerged in the context of this world of sensible sex, a nightmare underlying our newfound rationality. The effect of all this porn should be enormously negative. The old second-wave feminist dictum "Pornography is the theory, and rape is the practice" is still largely accepted. There were extensive studies into the effect of pornography on individuals during the so-called feminist sex wars of the 1980s and 1990s. In one early study, undertaken in 1982, researchers at the University of Indiana asked 160 undergraduates to watch a series of films. Some sat through standard educational or entertainment material, but others saw short movies that contained "fellatio, cunnilingus, coition, and anal intercourse." One group saw six porn films a week, for a period of six weeks—a total of almost five hours of sexually explicit material. After completing this porn marathon, the students were asked to read a newspaper account of a man who picked up and raped a female hitchhiker. They learned from the story that the man had been convicted and were asked to suggest a suitable sentence for his crime. Men who had seen the mainstream movies wanted to jail the rapist for almost eight years; those who watched the sex scenes suggested a sentence just over half as long. Exposure to large amounts of pornography, the researchers concluded, "trivializes rape through the portrayal of women as hyperpromiscuous and socially irresponsible."

Other researchers interviewed rapists and found that the effects implied by the Indiana study appear to apply to real life. One team, who talked to 341 sex offenders, found that pornography "added significantly to the prediction of recidivism." Another group discovered that many convicted rapists had been exposed to hard-core pornography before high school. One rapist told a researcher that after watching a pornographic film: "That's when I started having rape fantasies. . . . I just went for it, went out and raped."

These results have been replicated numerous times in the past thirty years, and the arguments for the dangers of pornography have formed into a coherent whole. In her 2012 book, *Violence and the Pornographic Imaginary*, the sociologist Natalie Purcell provides a summary: "Exposure to pornography has . . . been linked to alarming attitudes toward women, toward sexual violence, and toward rape victims. Several studies suggest that one's level of exposure to pornography is positively correlated with acceptance of 'rape myths' and victim-blaming attitudes or beliefs that trivialize rape. The most disturbing studies on exposure to sexually explicit material suggest that self-reported level of pornography exposure is related to history of rape and propensity to rape." Given that every man on earth has been exposed to this imagery, much of which is violent, we should in theory be terrified for the future of the world's sexual practices. If nearly every boy and man is exposed to violent pornography, and pornography leads to sexual violence, then the flood of pornography with which the Internet floods male consciousness should lead to an epidemic of rape and sexual violence.

Except that the opposite happens. As early as 2006 the economist Todd Kendall conducted a state-by-state study comparing high-speed Internet access and rape rates. He concluded that "a 10 percentage point increase in Internet access is associated with a decline in reported rape victimization of around 7.3 percent." The Kendall study does not directly connect the use of porn with lower rape rates, only high-speed Internet access and rape. High-speed Internet access doesn't correspond to any other declining crime rates, however. Also, the decline of the rape rate corresponds exactly to those groups—that is, fourteen- to eighteen-year-olds—for whom Internet pornography represents the greatest leap in ease of access. Kendall suggests pornography is a "substitute" for rape.

Studies conducted before the rise of the Internet found no connection between pornography and rape. In 1991 Berl Kutchinsky of the Institute of Criminal Science at the University of Copenhagen undertook a broad study in Denmark, Sweden, and West Germany during the period 1964–84. The availability of pornography, including violent pornography, in those countries rose dramatically over that time. Yet in none of the countries did rape increase more than nonsexual violent crimes. "This finding in itself would seem sufficient to discard the hypothesis that pornography causes rape," concluded Kutchinsky.

A team that studied pornography access and sex crimes in Japan found an inverse correlation: "The number and availability of sexually explicit materials increased in Japan over the years 1972–95. At the same time, the incidence of rape declined from 4,677 cases with 5,464 offenders in 1972 to 1,500 cases with 1,160 offenders in 1995." Pornography had an even more marked effect on juvenile sexual assault rates.

A pornography paradox is emerging: When huge quantities of violent sexual imagery flood male consciousness, real sexual violence either stays the same or declines.

*   *   *

The antipornography crusades in Iceland and Britain are not empirically based attempts to decrease sexual violence against women. They are moral panics. They indulge a visceral but in-substantial outrage, the widespread lament "What is happening to men?" Specifically "What is happening to young men?" In the past the same crude fear and self-righteous piety we see today in the attacks against porn manifested in attempts to curb rap music and video games. The underlying assumption in all these debates has remained ludicrously simplistic: representations of violence are violence, and representations of violence lead to violence.

Andrea Dworkin, the gender theorist whose explosive work on pornography in the early 1970s began the sex wars, was the first writer to frame pornography as a feminist moral issue: "The major theme of pornography as a genre is male power, its nature, its magnitude, its use, its meaning." Her hatred of male power consumed her, and ultimately consumed the debate around pornography. Her enemies were not in error; they were evil. Her Pornography Resource Center staged "porn drives" in which women smuggled porn out of their homes. When one woman set herself on fire in protest against porn, the PRC compared her to the anti-Vietnam protester Norman Morrison and claimed her self-immolation was "an act of political protest" undertaken in the name of women living "under conditions of political and sexual terrorism."

The rise of radical feminism was a "great awakening" in tune with the other great religious revivals of American history. Campaigns against "demon rum" are the direct ancestors of the campaigns against "demon porn." When Dworkin lectured, one spectator later wrote, "her left arm shook in the air, tears stained the spaces around her eyes into violet saucers."

Moral panic over male sexuality predates the rise of modern pornography by millennia. The Zohar makes onanism a worse crime than murder, and for Christians masturbation was a mortal sin, both an unnatural act and one condemned by scripture. Jean Stengers and Anne Van Neck's *Masturbation: The History of a Terror* collects these moral panics, each abetted by horrific stories about the outcome of masturbation. There is the story of two onanists in the *Bonum Universale de Apibus* by Thomas of Cantimpré, an allegorical social commentary from the thirteenth century: "One of these unfortunates died while screaming, 'May God's vengeance be upon me! May God's vengeance be upon me!' God's anger, in the face of this abject sin, manifested itself not only through divine retribution but through miracles, which functioned as so many warnings. It is thus, he told us, that a masturbator, having tried, with guilty intentions, to grasp his penis, suddenly felt a snake in his hand. Thomas abominated 'the heinousness of this sin.' "

The religious loathing of masturbation was transferred into a secular framework during the Enlightenment. Samuel-August Tissot's *L'Onanisme* was hugely popular in the eighteenth century, going through hundreds of reprints and many translations. Tissot, a physician, claimed, "This deadly habit kills more youth than all diseases combined." His list of the side effects of masturbation included loss of memory, dementia, anxiety, "continual anguish," dizzy spells, weakening of all senses, insomnia and nightmares, coughing fits, low fevers, consumption, headaches and stomach pains, rheumatism, pimples,

gonorrhea, priapism, tumors of the testes, sterility, constipa-
tion, diarrhea, and hemorrhoids. Thus the need for preventative
undergarments, for "toothed urethral rings," for bells attached
to penises which tinkled at erections.

The abjection of male desire was by no means the invention
of radical feminists on New York street corners in the 1970s. It
was a commonplace of medical literature for most of history in
the Christian West. The strength and depth of that abjection
is visible in the strong resistance the group of researchers who
founded the *Journal of Porn Studies* in England has endured.
Before a single article had been presented, its potential existence provoked wild fury; the group Stop Porn Culture accused
them of being "promoters of porn culture." Gail Dines, the author of *Pornland*, described the founders of the journal as "akin
to climate change deniers." Antiporn activists fear the moral
muddiness that knowledge inevitably brings, as all moralists
do. The connection the feminists against porn wish to draw
is simple: Image leads to the perversion of male desire, which
leads to violent men, which leads to violence against women
generally. A "Journal of Porn Culture" will naturally problema-
tize and complicate and blur every line in that diagram. That's
what scholarship does.

For a force so utterly transformative, the research we currently have, though full of fascinating hints, is sketchy and incomplete. Research into pornography has so far suffered from
several discrete problems, some methodological, some social.
Old-fashioned moral prurience stigmatizes it. The technological novelty is confusing. We don't really know what the Internet

is doing to us; how can we know what the combination of sex and the Internet is doing to us? And then Internet pornography itself is in a state of intense flux, changing month by month. Research into Internet porn, in short, is like trying to hit a moving target in the dark with your eyes half-closed.

The empirical evidence we do have about pornography is confusing, not just the evidence on violence. For example, it is a truism that pornography corrodes the capacity for sexual and personal intimacy. But a recent study comparing the answers of 164 men to the Perceived Interpersonal Closeness Scale and the Pornography Use Information Questionnaire found "no definite link between the self-reported use of pornography and perceived interpersonal closeness." Instead the study found that "pornography use was not just an escape from intimacy but also an expression of the search for it." Even sexual permissiveness, which correlates with greater pornography use, is subject to all kinds of factors besides mere exposure. In a 2013 report self-described liberals grew significantly more sexually permissive after watching porn, while self-described conservatives grew slightly less permissive. The report's conclusion? "Preexisting beliefs moderate the attitudinal application of activated sexual scripts." If the effects of watching porn depend on something as vague as the political views of its spectators, what other possible factors might apply?

It only gets more confusing. In one study of teenagers' use of pornography and its relationship to their sexual development, the researchers could find few correlations of any kind. The porn itself didn't seem to matter so much as the context of the person consuming the porn. If we are not capable of judging pornography by its effects, then by what standard are we to judge it?

The deeper the research into Internet pornography, the less confident, the more tentative the conclusions become. The crudity of abjection remains. The political debate is at present a thoughtless return to primordial fear of the brutality of male libido. This fear, and the pseudo-morality that seizes upon it, prevents us from seeing how culture and politics and economics modulate the link, if any, between pornography and sexual violence. The simplistic idea that porn causes sexual violence, promoted by radical conservatives and radical feminists alike, obscures the issue. Fear prevents us from thinking.

* * *

Not that fear is an inappropriate response to Internet pornography. The sheer disgust porn creates is entirely understandable; indeed disgust itself is one of the primary experiences of its consumers. In her book on pornography, Dworkin's first example is an issue of *Penthouse* with women splayed on trucks like shot deer. Compared to what is currently available, women as corpses seems naïvely sweet. It's almost pastoral.

The scope and intensity of Internet pornography is shocking. And being shocked is part of the experience. You may enjoy watching busty blondes giving blowjobs, but shemales are there too. As are women splayed in Mengele-style medical equipment, women with their faces covered in the cum of a hundred men, cartoon monster porn, stepfather-stepdaughter sex. Any given viewer of Pornhub is at the very least aware that millions and millions of his fellow men want to see incestuous acts simulated. And those are the videos on free porn sites, sites that are intended as teasers for the truly hard-core material that has to be paid for. Never mind the material that is illegal.

The porn habits of men are bizarre, even in the tangential, partial picture we currently have. The most popular porn star in the world, by far, according to Pornhub's Insight research page, is forty-two-year-old Lisa Ann. Individuals tend to search for women of their own nationality. In the United States *ebony* is the most popular search term, after *massage*. PornMD provides a live stream of searches on its various free websites. It's a sometimes chilling, sometimes bizarre point of access to male sexuality. Sometimes it's funny: My Little Pony pornography is most popular in Belarus and Russia. Here's a list of the terms viewers were searching during the three minutes I spent on the site: *youth, ember, massage creep, sorority hazing fuck, horse and girl, german rough pis* [sic]*, pleasant anal, hungry grandmas, deepthroat gag choke punk, hijab, diaper, prostate blow job, mom son porn ebony, eat dung, wetplay gay marie, man, Japanese invisible man, hot girl panty pooping, Russian money, big ass little guy, African native tribes, welsh, granny squirter, casting road sex, milk enema, snake sex, Bengali muslim, gynecology model, iceporn taboo, red bone sleeping underwear, huge cartoon cock, public humility, fuck the librarian.* That's three minutes. Male desire is a shape-shifting beast. The male gaze has absolutely nothing to do with the pretty pictures in *Vogue.*

Consumers of pornography have a line they will not cross—or perhaps one they flirt with crossing. It's a key component of every man's experience of Internet pornography: I enjoy this, but *that* is reprehensible. The line is more or less arbitrary, though felt deeply. Sexual identity becomes a series of negations: I am not the kind of guy who wears sunglasses while screwing. I am not the kind of guy who chokes women. I am not the kind of guy who likes to watch women get fucked by donkeys. Masculine desire becomes a map with missing margins: beyond that line there be dragons. And in some cases the monsters are literal. In Japan "tentacle rape porn," women violated by squidlike monsters, is increasingly popular. Here we have the pornographic imagination in its most complete, perfect expression: degradation by the abyss.

What are we looking at when we look at pornography? What exactly are we exposing ourselves to? Pornography is famously indefinable, which may explain why its content is so easy to ignore. The narratives in pornography are famously irrelevant, the man who reads *Playboy* for the articles a stock figure of the sexual liar. In *Boogie Nights* the porn film director played by Burt Reynolds dreams of making a film with enough suspense that the viewers stay after they've come. Nonetheless, before the Internet almost all pornography in magazines and videos had story lines—that's why *Penthouse* had women hanging from trees and Santa Claus penetrating the elves and so on. Nudity is only half of pornography, the pleasure of the flesh. The story lines of pornography offer a vision of the world sexualized, a world in which every situation can be turned into an opportunity for intercourse: pizza delivery, soccer games, classic novels, the Supreme Court. Pornography creates an alternate universe of quasi-infinite sexual plenty.

Today narratives of this type survive only in the "classier" productions of the larger companies, like Vivid or Hustler. Since pornography long ago exhausted most settings, the story lines tend to be super topical, drawn from the news or parodies of hit movies and television shows. The stories need only to be stories, but the stories are as important as the naked bodies. They declare, "The world is there to be fucked."

The Internet has accelerated the metabolism of pornography. The Internet vaporizes, atomizes: online porn is free and instantly accessible, more extreme, with less context. Narrative persiflage diminishes. Internet pornography, and digital pornography that preceded it on DVD, is mostly gonzo. It is composed of single scenes, separated from the others, often categorized by fetish: Anal Sluts #19, Bad Babysitters #17. On a site like Pornhub the thousands of videos are moderated only by search terms and by the name of the performer. The vagueness hides the narrative. The narrative within the videos parallels the narrative of the performer's career and also the narrative of the consumer of pornography. The individual scenes move from teasing to whatever sexual act is slated for performance to the inevitable cumshot. The women go from nude poses to solo poses to blowjobs to regular sex to double penetration to gangbangs to a world of vicarious degradation that's nearly infinite in its elaboration. In each case there is an arc of increasing degradation.

This degradation works on a self-feeding loop. The description of Hugh Hefner's orgies from Izabella St. James's *Bunny Tales* is a litany of this agony of desensitization. The Wednesday and Friday night group-sex sessions at the Mansion had a set pattern. Hef had sex with four girls at a time, for about two minutes apiece, while his "main girlfriend," Holly, organized everything, wiping his penis off in between: "After that came (no pun intended) the grand finale: Hef masturbated while watching the porn, and Holly sucked on his nipple, trying to spread herself all over him so that no one else had physical contact with him during the moment of his ultimate ecstasy. I never saw him come while having sex with anyone; he *always* masturbated. And it was always the same: too much baby oil, his hand, and the visual support of porn or the better alternative of a couple of the girls making out." This scene is the nightmare at the bottom of pornography, the frozen erotic lake where Judas is devoured by Satan. Medicated, surrounded by identical pneumatic women, swamped by plastic flesh, able to orgasm only by his own hand—what could be more grotesque or less erotic? What scene could demonstrate the decline of human sexuality into empty pantomime more entirely? It's a warning, that scene, a warning that sexual novelty can devolve into ever-failing attempts to outflank our own craving for tenderness.

The narrative arc of Internet pornography ends in the display of cum every time—this is the key to understanding its power. The cumshot is the real difference between pornography and fleshly sexuality: you cannot make yourself come by watching yourself come in real life. The cumshot is the essence of the pornographic process, the marking of the particular feminine reality by the generalized goo of indistinct masculine spirit. What happens with the cum is the absolute first descriptive marker of the category of pornography. Cream pie. Tits. Belly. Feet. Is it a gesture of dominance or the simulation of a woman taking pleasure in the production of semen? Or both?

Every scene in Kink.com, the world's most popular BDSM site, begins with an image of the woman, about to be degraded, smiling. That is the story of all Internet pornography, the key to its significance and a narrative wildly different from the earlier, softer narratives found in *Penthouse* and *Hustler*; it is male power over women right along the line of consent, threatening always to slip over. Every pornographer knows somebody who "hates women," but it's not them, not them. No, it's somebody else. The women all *consent* to be powerless. That contradiction is the core of all pornographic expression on the Internet. The subject of Internet pornography is the acceptance of the force of male desire.

Intriguingly, women's erotica contains the same contradictions. In " 'She Exploded into a Million Pieces': A Qualitative and Quantitative Analysis of Orgasms in Contemporary Romance Novels," researchers at the University of Ottawa found exactly the same sense of violence in erotic fiction marketed to women: "Many orgasm descriptions contained images referring to violence and death. In fact almost half of coded extracts (42%) contained references to this theme. Orgasms were associated with breaking, shattering, ripping, and exploding of the characters' bodies. . . . Depictions of romance novel orgasms were often characterized by a sense that the character had become involuntarily vulnerable during climax. Over half of orgasm descriptions (52%) reflected this theme." *Fifty Shades of Grey*, a book so successful it led to the unprecedented act by a publishing company of delivering bonus checks to every employee, is one long story of the consent to powerlessness, of a woman taken to the edge of the meaning of consent. Most of the book is the negotiation of a contract between Anastasia Steele and Christian Grey. Hot sex is bureaucratic, and the paperwork involves Anastasia enslaving herself, giving away all control over her body, even over what she eats. And this is erotica aimed at women, remember. If governments are going to restrict male pornography, they should consider restricting *Fifty Shades of Grey* too. One is images, the other is words, but both contain the same vision of sexual desire: women who want to be shattered, who consent to be powerless.

* * *

Consent is the real subject of our sexual obsession. Straight pornography is only tangentially about the flesh; its proper subject is female submission. That obsession does not necessarily imply that pornography is a rejection of the newly emerging consent-based morality that defines postfeminist, post–gay rights sexual politics. Quite the opposite. When consent is the sole standard of what is sexually taboo, it should come as no surprise that consent becomes the all-consuming libidinal focus.

Internet pornography is no freak against egalitarian politics but a result of their triumph. And it always has been. His-
torically and intellectually pornography coincides with the
empowerment of women. The most patriarchal countries in
the world are the ones that ban pornography, exactly because
pornography threatens patriarchy. Under patriarchy women's
sexuality is men's property. In pornography women's sexuality
is a commodity women can exchange for other items of value.
The Marquis de Sade wrote his fantasies of degradation in a
period of French history that has been called "the golden age of
women," when independent *salonistes* like Julie de Lespinasse
and Josephine were celebrated for their intellectual and social
power. De Sade, who was at the financial mercy of his wife and
mother for most of his life, created pornography in the context
of such dependence. After the Second World War pornography
became most prevalent in the most egalitarian societies, notably
in Scandinavia. The first producer of high-quality color hard-
core films, distinct from stag movies, was Lasse Braun, an Ital-
ian making films in Sweden, then the world's foremost example
of gender equality. From Sweden and later from Denmark the
kind of visual pornography we know today spread to America.
The rise of pornography in Western Europe and America coincided with the rise of women in the workplace.

Pornography could be taken as a backlash against feminism. Men, confronted by powerful women in real life, hu-
miliate them in their fantasies, or so the argument goes. I
think this would be a misreading of the reaction, which is less
a backlash than a deflection. If you want to understand how

men work, go to any large porn site around Easter: elaborate pink borders with eggs and bunnies decorate the website. They sell a cornucopia of sexual horrors, but they see no reason not to spruce up their foyer, like a grocery store, like a car dealership. They want their anal violations to look nice and be in keeping with the season. Men go to Internet porn because to them it isn't about women; it's about product. Men who would never go to a prostitute go to Internet porn. Men who would never go to a strip club go to Internet porn. The ethics of the production are gruesome, of course, although as much for the male as the female performers, who often earn as little as a hundred dollars a shoot. Besides, who demands products that are ethically manufactured? Certainly nobody who wants cocaine. Nobody who wants furniture or clothes, either. In the current state of capitalism, all logistical chains are morally suspect. To have a conscience and to eat you have to forget where the food comes from. The same is true for porn.

* * *

David Cameron—who, again, may or may not have had sex with a dead pig—claims that porn pollutes the Internet. He couldn't be more wrong. Porn is the avatar of the Internet, its metaphoric self-expression. Porn is more entwined with the technical means of its dissemination than any other content. Porn fulfills the destiny of the screen itself.

The screen has always been as much about the flight to intimacy as the flight from intimacy. The original cinemas reduced whole crowds into passive recipients of projected image, but the experience from the very beginning was understood as a kind of collective erotic rapture. In those dark rooms people were all the same and yet alone, their ecstasy a mass connection composed of utter isolation. The movie stars possessed the crowds and were possessed by them at the same moment; we gave to this communion the name of glamour. The screen reflects back the desires projected onto it. And there is always an edge of dissatisfaction to what should be a perfect reflection, the echo of Narcissus. Glamour is never satisfying or sufficient.

So powerful was the screen, so efficiently calibrated to the substructures of consciousness, that its presence has expanded endlessly since its invention. These are twin laws of the twenty-first century: Anywhere a screen can go it will go. Anywhere a screen is, porn is. The intermediation of projected images floods consciousness like liquid into a container that expands as it is filled. The dark rooms are everywhere now. Every room of the house is a dark room. Every person on the street carries a dark room in his or her pocket.

The screens connect us by being between us. Porn is the sexual reality that emerges out of that contradictory function. By allowing for a space for the projection of desire, rationality about sexuality converts sex into a consumerist commodity, but the desires being projected turn out to be monstrous because the rationality creates the hunger to pass beyond it. The intermediation of the screen, which creates the space for sensible decisions, also creates a distance that its sensible decision makers long to cross. The other instances of screened sexuality, whether Tinder or Grindr or OKCupid, have the same combination of the sensible and the shocking. Why else would men send women pictures of their dicks? In the matrices of swipes and clicks, the negotiations of various status markers, where the other can delete your file, the dickpic is a taboo violation, the primordial boast. Here's my cock. Love it.

Sex itself has never been easier than now. Sex has never been healthier or more open or more available. Sex has never been, in a word, more negotiable. As a result sex doesn't matter as much.* Thus the peculiar melancholy that haunts the hedonists of our moment. I've known many men who've slept with hundreds of women, but almost none who are happy about it, even fewer who are stupid enough to be proud of the fact. Sleeping with hundreds is much easier than sleeping with one, and we all know it.

The most expensive package prostitutes sell is the GFE, the girlfriend experience, which involves cuddling, kissing, the pretense of a relationship, the hard-to-fake pleasures of intimacy.

---

*Steve is, of course, speaking here about post-Enlightenment contemporary Western culture. Sex is only healthy and open when you are lucky enough to live in a culture where sex is healthy and open. In Toronto at the moment the public schools have introduced a progressive sex ed curriculum that includes homosexuality as just another way to be, and some parents—mostly Muslim and Christian— are pulling their kids out of public schools as a result. We see such culture clashes happening across the Western world. It is not clear, at least not to me, that we won't regress.

Tenderness is more expensive than anal. Which makes sense: it's rarer, more complicated, more desirable. Physical acts grow more and more extreme in the pursuit of something that physical love can only hint at.

* * *

Diogenes the Cynic masturbated in the marketplace and called it philosophy. Of all the wisdom available in ancient Athens, his was the earthiest, the most practical. He refused to condemn the body out of social propriety. If he was built to ejaculate, he should ejaculate, and therefore he ejaculated where everyone could see him. The Athenians loved him for his frankness, which provoked laughter as much as disgust. When asked why he masturbated in public, he answered, "Would that by rubbing my belly I could get rid of hunger." Diogenes offered the pagan view of masturbation: Why be ashamed of the easiest expression of masculine desire? Why fear the erasure of male sexual appetite by the lightest, the most harmless of gestures?

The rise of Internet pornography is a symptom more than a cause, a symptom of egalitarianism itself, a method of dealing with the embarrassment of male sexual power in the context of gender equality. The idea that porn has produced sexual objectification of women is staggeringly naïve, really too obtuse to be considered seriously. Go and watch a movie from the pre-porn era and see. James Bond didn't care too scrupulously for consent. The hero of *Alfie*, that fabulous missive from the beginning of the sexual revolution, looks in the light of the present like a rampant sexual terrorist. He had no pornography. He called women "it." Sexual objectification exists in all times and all places. Modern pornography exists in worlds where women have power, exactly where they cannot be objectified in real life.

The mechanism at work in Internet pornography and in *Fifty Shades of Grey* is a classic case of repression. Michel Foucault identified a nearly identical mechanism in nineteenth-century sexual morality, with its discursive transposition of sexual language into what he called "polymorphous incitement." The restrictive morality of the nineteenth century conjured a sexualized world. Most notably homosexual acts, which had once been mere acts, became markers of identity. Everything became sexualized: when you cannot say "the leg of a table" because it is too suggestive and must instead say "the limb of a table," even the furniture is sexy. The definitive icon of Victorian England, after Victoria herself, is Jack the Ripper. They reflect each other. They need each other to exist. They are the result of each other. Every Doctor Jekyll makes his Mister Hyde. The size of the monstrosity reveals the size of the repression and the size of the virtue.

Just as the repression of sex in the nineteenth century spawned a vast array of perversions and an immense business class to service those perversions, so the repressions implicit in the morality of consent have generated a vast array of new perversions in our own time. How could it be any other way? We want equality, but sex is not equal. We want justice, but desire is not just. Nobody fucks justly. Andrea Dworkin once wrote that the only possible egalitarian sexuality between a man and a woman involved a limp penis:

> *I suggest to you that transformation of the male sexual model under which we now all labor and "love" begins where there is a congruence, not a separation, a congruence of feeling and erotic interest; that it begins in what we do know about female sexuality as distinct from male—clitoral touch and sensitivity all over the body (which needn't—and shouldn't—be localized or contained genitally), in tenderness, in self-respect and in absolute mutual respect. For me I suspect that this transformation begins in the place they most dread—that is, in a limp penis. I think that men will have to give up their precious erections and begin to make love as women do together.*

She was mocked for that comment, but it was her most essential insight. A fourteen-year-old with a stiff prick is the living refutation of the Enlightenment. He is an end in himself with an object attached to him. Of all the great feminist philosophers, Dworkin is the one who is most of our moment. What if she was right?

Dworkin's anger is of very little use to real people, but that doesn't mean she was wrong. The profundity of the feminist cause makes its achievement ultimately impossible. Dworkin wrote, "Under patriarchy, no woman is safe to live her life, or to love, or to mother children. Under patriarchy, every woman is a victim, past, present, and future. Under patriarchy, every woman's daughter is a victim, past, present, and future. Under patriarchy, every woman's son is her potential betrayer and also the inevitable rapist or exploiter of another woman." She loved mothers and daughters but hated procreation—this is honesty. No matter how triumphant the revolution, no matter how fair the laws, no matter how cleaned up the culture, at the end we are going to be left with male and female bodies and their desires, which are brutal. We all struggle with an irreconcilable contradiction: the pursuit of justice and the pursuit of sexual satisfaction. At the very least we have to acknowledge the possibility that the two are simply incompatible. Nobody so far has solved human desire.

Freud understood that the repression of the libido is the source of civilization. The torment of sexual joy is the main insight of psychoanalysis. We should not be surprised that when we curb male sexuality, as we want to, as we need to, the repressed desire will explode in subterranean fantasies. This process has been understood in the broadest terms for at least a century. If you are civilized, you will create monsters. The monstrosity of pornography is a sign of how civilized we have become.

Between barbarism and civilization, between the wilderness and the law, between the basic unfairness of our bodies and the hope of justice, the intricacies of sexual power and the purity of consent, we struggle to build a life. These struggles will not end if pornography is stripped from the Internet. Silent horror and shaming disgust at male sexuality—Internet porn as "pollution"—cannot be correct responses. We need culture, not piety.

Diogenes brought masturbation into the marketplace, but he also related the story of its origin. The god Hermes taught his son Pan to masturbate to ease the pain of his love for Echo. Pan taught the technique to the lonely shepherds. Masturbation is thus a gift from the gods, like fire, like wine. Maybe that's all civilization is: a bunch of tricks. Internet porn is just the latest.

FIVE

—

Against Outrage

MAYBE we are between civilizations. The old civilization of male dominance is crumbling under the weight of its absurdity, and the new civilization based on gender equality is ever so slowly rising. The contradictions of the transition torture us; they make us look gross and ridiculous. Intellectual and moral confusion is the natural condition of contemporary gender experience, a confusion we are all constantly trying to suppress and avoid.

This confusion is the stuff of everyday life. Sometimes it can arise from nothing more than silly incongruities. I heard a rumor not long ago that the woman who gave me my first blowjob was about to be named a judge. (It was just a rumor, it turned out.) We lost touch after high school, but I had followed the rapid rise of her career, as you do with people you once crouched with in the ragged patch of adolescent poplars. She had always been brilliant, even when she was sixteen. It was no big deal. But the idea was intensely strange to me, at least momentarily.

Later I was visiting an old friend who teaches sociology at a small university in rural Ontario. We were watching our kids on the playground—my son wrestling in the grass with some boy he'd run into, her daughter sitting in a circle of girls quietly decorating a sandcastle with pinecones. We started chatting about how stark the differences between boys and girls can be, and how unexpected. It's biological, she said, it has to be—a comment I found funny from a sociologist. You say that to your colleagues? I asked. I don't, she said, smiling. At home it's biological. At the university it's all structure.

Later still I was at a bachelor party, one of those bizarre rituals in which men have to stoop to their stereotype as a kind of recognition of common brutality, and we were all drunkenly heading to a strip club when my wife called. She needed to talk. A man she worked with called her "Honey."* It pissed

---

*That guy, several decades my senior, was sexist in a subtle, paternalistic way common to his generation. To his credit he was encouraging of my work. He set high expectations for me. We spoke frankly with each other, and he respected my opinions. But unlike the men my age, who grew up with feminism, he would often draw attention to people's gender; he'd refer to the "gentlemen," the "ladies," the "tough broads," and yes, he called me "Honey." He once said a high-ranking female staffer sounded "shrill." He made a big fuss of complimenting women in the office who dressed up. And here is the advice he gave me, based, I believe, on a sincere, good-natured desire to help me in my career: He told me that I should wear brighter clothes. He told me I should smile more. And, even more objectionably, he told me I should talk less. He actually said, "You have two ears and one mouth," a phrase so antiquated I had to Google it.

her off. It pissed me off. It pissed me off that this classic old-school garbage should survive. And so I found myself enraged, genuinely enraged at the sexism of a world that would call my wife "Honey" just as I was entering a business in which I was going to pay to see women naked.

Such are the everyday minor anti-epiphanies of living through the twenty-first-century rearrangement of gender. They subtract from rather than add to what I thought I knew about myself and others. It would be possible in each case to tease out the strands of the contradiction, to say "Here is adolescent sex, and here is the majesty of law. Here is child rearing, and here is the theory of gender. Here is the powerful woman you love, and here is your brute nature." The reality seems so much more manageable when separated, and it's tempting to believe that only the juxtapositions produce the sense of confusion. The point is that the way we live now inevitably puts those juxtapositions in our way. The rearrangement is messy. And the messiest part is that these

---

I was embarrassed and outraged, and, to my surprise, I also pitied him a little because he seemed so out of touch. Needless to say, no one ever tells men they should smile more. I told a female colleague about the advice I had received, and we agreed that there was truth to it, that powerful women often accomplish more if they sugarcoat things. Then, in a moment so intimate I can barely stand to remember it, my colleague started to cry. Women have come so far—and yet the workplace still demands that we mask our power, tone down our strength, act feminine, girly, unthreatening to the men above us on the food chain.

anti-epiphanies—crumbling ideals, devastated orders—are obviously the moments of maturity.

The messiness of personal politics in our time and place leads, organically, to a state of intellectual and moral hyper-certainty, of gender fanaticism—there is on the one hand, the social justice warriors and on the other hand, men's rights activists. As the experience of being men and women has become more fraught and complicated, the reaction to that experience has become more simplistic and shrill. And the smaller the matter at hand, the shriller the response. Outrage is the automatic response to any subject that falls under the rubric "The personal is political," whether it's pornography or housework or what shoes women wear or conversations at parties. The outrage serves mainly to obviate the contradictions that are the substance of our moment, to make its proponents look virtuous.

The deep irony of our moment is that, as historical forces beyond anybody's control bring men and women closer together, the way we talk about men and women remains resolutely divisive and despairing. The classic human instinct to retreat into oversimplification when confronted by a complex new reality is only a partial explanation. There is also a failure of theory. The intersection of the personal and the political has devolved into moralism, attenuated from facts and self-consuming in its pursuit of ideological purity. Outrage cannot help us understand the new intimacies and the new politics that emerge from the new intimacies.

In that strip club with my brother and his friends, I was

talking with one of the naked women, who had come up to try to make me spend twenty dollars to writhe her ass on my thighs for the length of an AC/DC song. A fleet of men in wheelchairs passed by. "Do you get a lot of handicapped guys?" I asked her, for something to ask. She sipped a twelve-dollar vodka tonic I had paid for. "One thing I've learned in this job is that we're all handicapped," she told me for free.

*　*　*

"The personal is political" was coined, as so many dubious yet enduring phrases were, in the late 1960s. Carol Hanisch, a pioneer in the women's liberation movement, wrote the essay of that title as a memorandum on various sessions she had attended with other "movement women" in New York and Gainesville, Florida. In 1969, women in groups discussing their personal struggles as political issues was a radical experiment, akin to acid tests or happenings, perhaps even more radical than those other attempts at the expansion of consciousness, since the women's sessions drilled into the motives of individual lives and the substructures of social arrangements.

The defensive tone of the essay can be startling, since from our own historical perspective its basic assumptions seem so obvious—that domestic and cultural questions are as vital as explicitly political questions—but it's also a testament to the strength of the essay. The ideas contained in "The Personal Is Political," which seemed borderline crazy when written, are now taken for granted.

I believe at this point, and maybe for a long time to come, that these analytical sessions are a form of political action. I do not go to these sessions because I need or want to talk about my "personal problems." In fact, I would rather not. As a movement woman, I've been pressured to be strong, self-less, other-oriented, sacrificing, and in general pretty much in control of my own life. To admit to the problems in my life is to be deemed weak. So I want to be a strong woman, in movement terms, and not admit I have any real problems that I can't find a personal solution to (except those directly related to the capitalist system). It is at this point a political action to tell it like it is, to say what I really believe about my life instead of what I've always been told to say.

A profound suspicion motivated "The Personal Is Political," a suspicion of hypocritical and willful ignorance. While movement women struggled for civil rights, the overthrow of the capitalist system, and the end of the Vietnam War, the men whose struggle they shared expected them to be sexually and domestically docile. In her conversations with ordinary women Hanisch saw that the machinery of gender politics doesn't run merely through legal and political institutions or factories; it runs through the entire fabric of society: in bed, in the kitchen, in the grocery story, in advertising, in magazines, and in movies.

The argument could have stopped there. Hanisch could merely have pointed out another species of oppression and rested. But she went further. She reflected the insight back at herself, to question her own motives and the nature of the movement to which she was devoted. She had self-identified as a "political woman," but what did it mean to be political if politics existed as a fragment of exterior life? "I think 'apolitical' women are not in the movement for very good reasons," she wrote, "and as long as we say 'you have to think like us and live like us to join the charmed circle,' we will fail. What I am trying to say is that there are things in the consciousness of 'apolitical' women (I find them very political) that are as valid as any political consciousness we think we have." This insight requires guts and humility to make. Not only was Hanisch rejecting the Marxist category of materialist struggle, the cornerstone of left-wing politics for a century, but she also cut through the question of style, the question of the political pose. Her politics were not radical chic. The opposite: for her the struggle belonged to the suburban housewife as much as to the Black Panther. From that humility, from that gesture of empathy to the struggles of those who were not like her and did not share her beliefs, Hanisch leaped into a politics as transcendent as it was quotidian, grand in outlook but minutely focused on the daily business of life.

"The Personal Is Political" began as a plea for more complexity, an appeal to widen the ground of feminism to include women who did not call themselves feminists, to look at the entire theater of gender relations. The concept vastly extended the field of thought for feminism; women's liberation was no longer the dry business of bills making their way through Congress, or amendments to the Constitution, or even equal pay for equal work. The dominant questions were domestic or sexual: the division of housework, violence against women. A world in which women are raped and beaten with impunity is not a liberated one, even if women have the vote.

The essay implied that all personal decisions—what to eat, what to wear, what to read, what to watch—were political decisions. Signs of male power could be found everywhere in the culture to those with the eyes to see. Inevitably that extension of critique involved a diffusion of its direction. The movement shifted from large actions at large institutions, which were few and obviously vital, to critiquing the constant barrage of misogyny. Thus the turn to the fashion industry and the medical profession. Thus *Ms.* magazine. Thus "fat is a feminist issue." Thus *The Beauty Myth*.

The ferocious brand of identity politics that arrived in the 1990s was little more than an extrapolation of "The Personal Is Political," a potential politicization of all aspects of human expression, from piercings to musical styles, from the consumption of meat to characters in vampire shows. As gender politics extended to embrace every aspect of life, the symptoms of oppression were omnipresent and the source of oppression grew vaguer: patriarchy or some other indefinable concept. The structure of privilege explained all differences, and this structure was taken as given, immemorial, unchanging. Gender politics became afflicted with the oversimplification that afflicts all personal morality: who suffers most is most virtuous. University departments blossomed into the pursuit of panvictimology. A hierarchy of impotence imposed itself.

Power was itself a moral failure, and those who came from powerlessness were inherently closer to truth and justice. Validity narrowed and narrowed until it collapsed at the fact that speech itself is power.

The great intellectual advantage of academic identity politics is its simplicity. Panvictimology freezes every group, and every person in those groups, into appointed, unmoving circles of good and evil, defined by structures of privilege and their overthrow by the forces of progress. The development of panvictimology also had an underlying economic motive: its convenience. Rather than having to teach students a methodology or, even more grueling, a body of knowledge, professors merely had to impress an attitude on their students, the attitude of virtue. Then they could cop that attitude and apply it to any situation. Every undergraduate who has taken a course in the humanities understands at least superficially the notion of structures of privilege and understands how to pose correctly when confronted with these structures. (They always insist on replicating those structures in their own lives of course.)

The game is called Check Your Privilege. Another name for it might be Who Is More Righteous Than I? It's learned in college, but it's played mostly online. Internet discussion takes the insights found in "The Personal Is Political" and renders them null and void, one by one. The analysis of personal struggle is reduced to stylized masks. The concern for apolitical people, for the lives of those who don't care about gender politics, vanishes into a vague contempt. Openness and humility toward other modes of life collapse into the opinion echo chamber of like-minded gangs. Meanwhile hope for real change grows less and less relevant. Hashtag activism—utterly impotent—loses sight of everything other than its own brief speechifying.

* * *

When it comes to gender, the Internet is a big scolding machine. Any failure in navigating the most complex rearrangement of social existence in history will automatically be greeted with vast choruses of howls. The smallest questions bring the largest hate. The most vicious debate on the subject of gender over the past couple of years has been on the topic of representation in video game reviewing. A more negligible question is hard to imagine. There is the vital point of context, however; the online space is an environment of horrific, all-consuming, and almost unprecedented misogyny, and the desolation of digital feminism is an inevitable consequence of the climate in which it has arisen.

Online feminists are making their arguments while being chased from their homes by an onslaught of direct, personal attacks. Virtually every feminist scholar and female critic of any kind has to endure outright threats of physical harm. For raising her voice on the matter of video games, Brianna Wu had to move to an undisclosed location. For campaigning to have a woman on the British ten-pound note, Stella Creasy had to install a panic button in her home. For trying to run Reddit, Ellen Pao was swept away on a tide of abuse. The debate around gender online is not happening in a dignified arena where a healthy spirit of give-and-take meets with a community of like-minded truth-seekers. Who can feel intelligent empathy for a group (in this case men) constantly calling for your rape and murder?

And feminism—a female political agenda—is the only one worth taking seriously online. As for the men's rights crowd or the seduction artists' crowd, or The Red Pill sub on Reddit, or Milo Yiannopolous, or the alt right generally—none of them properly rise to the level of argument. They are expressions of pure hostility toward female independence as such, and are of interest only as anthropological phenomena. Intellectually they are literally beneath contempt; they have no ideas worth critiquing.

Men's rights groups have taken the identity politics of the 1990s and inverted it. Men are the victims now! Men are excluded from jobs because of their gender! Men are victimized because they do all the hard jobs! Men die earlier than women! The claim that straight men in the prosperous democracies today are victims is the sincerest form of flattery to radical feminists. How deeply those men must crave the moral certainties of being the downtrodden, the salve of the sense of injustice. That blind anger is true parochialism. The world doesn't need a men's movement. History has been the men's movement.

The setup is really closer to World of Warcraft—social justice warriors against trolls—than it is to a genuine debate. The problem is mistaking it for debate. Digital outrage is comically ephemeral in hindsight, but while it's happening the deadly earnestness of attitudinal politics can be unbearably oppressive, mainly by the absence of any larger perspective. The case of the feminist folk singer Ani DiFranco was unhappily instructive in the nature of this new virtue. Here is a woman who has devoted her life to progressive causes, who has made real sacrifices, refusing to sell herself to a record label, for example, and who is one of the very few singers under the age of seventy who has managed to write powerful songs on political subjects. None of this helped when the Internet discovered she had planned a "Righteous Retreat" on the site of the former Nottoway Plantation in Louisiana. The outrage went viral and global: how dare she make music in a place in the southern United States where there had once been slaves?

DiFranco apologized but made the mistake of trying to explain herself and to excuse her actions: "I did not imagine or understand that the setting of a plantation would trigger such collective outrage or result in so much high velocity bitterness. I imagined instead that the setting would become a participant in the event. This was doubtless to be a gathering of progressive and engaged people, so I imagine a dialogue would emerge organically over the four days about the issues of where we were." Her appeal to reason was a colossal tactical error. The devout cannot tolerate pride in their penitents. The outrage only went more viral, more global. The righteous demand abasement before they will permit readmission, and DiFranco gave it to them in her second apology: "It is obvious to me now that you were right; all those who said we can't in good conscience go to that place and support it or look past for one moment what it deeply represents. I needed a wake up call and you gave it to me." So the forces of righteousness had won and were satisfied.

Their not inconsiderable efforts had humiliated one of their staunchest activists. They had given Ani DiFranco a wake-up call. I am sure they felt good about themselves. I hope they did. What else could the point have been?

There is a small group of men who respond to panvictimology by trying to join in. They call themselves "male feminists." They launch websites. They speak and write, mostly about how shitty (other) men are. They go to rallies. Sometimes they even try to help organize these rallies. These men want to join in the struggle because they want the joy of hatefully overcoming, a form of angry pleasure often tinged with a distinct eroticism. They don't realize that they themselves, inevitably, will be turned into those who need to be overcome. Identity politics is not involved in the construction of productive allegiances based on the desire for similar goals. None of these groups is looking for allies; they all want enemies. A good enemy can manufacture an enormous amount of outrage.

The most famous of recent male feminists is Hugo Schwyzer, a former professor of gender studies at Pasadena City College and a blogger who wrote for *Jezebel* and the *Atlantic*. His prolific output of female-positive writings online did not prevent him from being called out for sleeping with students, sexting a twenty-seven-year-old porn star, and other examples of bad male behavior. Eventually the chorus of accusations from the women whose cause he so desperately wanted to join led to a form of intellectual suicide. He offered a Maoist-style self-criticism on Twitter, with over a hundred posts like "You can denounce me now, I'm out of feminism, not because I don't believe in it, but because I'm such a p***poor [*sic*] example of it." Then he checked himself into a psych ward.

Other so-called male feminists took his moment of collapse as a personal triumph and crowed gleefully online over his downfall. There's no better way to achieve ideological purity than to attack fellow travelers. The great Rabbi Hillel in the *Pirkei Avot* had a vision of self-consumption that fits neatly here: "He saw a skull floating on the surface of the water and he said unto it: Because you drowned others they drowned you; and those that drowned you will eventually be drowned." The hunger for outrage eventually turns on its neighbor, as it has in every ideology. There is always someone more oppressed than you, who can claim a more authentic position and who can find you a participant in the structure of privilege. Just being thin is enough.

One thing I learned from living through the political correctness of the 1990s is that, if you're a woman and you hear a man calling himself a feminist,* run, don't walk, away from that man. Jian Ghomeshi—who was acquitted after facing sexual assault charges by three women, and had a similar charge by yet another withdrawn in exchange for a peace bond

---

*I winced at first when I heard that Justin Trudeau, Canada's prime minister, referred to himself as a feminist at the Davos World Economic Forum (it seemed a little boastful), but if he has to use the word to make equality a front-burner issue, I'm all for it. And anyway, deeds are more important than words. He has put so many smart, qualified women on his cabinet, he could call himself a Mouseketeer for all I care.

and an apology for his sexually inappropriate behavior in the workplace—was an icon of the fine young upstanding male feminist. He graduated from York University, the most politically correct university in Canada—which is saying something—with a minor in women's studies. He even blurbed *The Guy's Guide to Feminism* as "an admirably accessible guide for guys to understand and embrace the other (often more incendiary) F-word. And it's even funny. Quite remarkable. Everyone knows feminists have no sense of humour!" His comment appeared alongside blurbs from Gloria Steinem and the editor of the online feminist site *Feministing*. And he turned out to be who he turned out to be. As people do.

The world doesn't need male feminists anyway. It needs decent guys.

* * *

The politics of intimacy has been hijacked by misogyny and outrage. We have lost ourselves in games of humiliation which deny us insight—the exact opposite of the original hope contained in "The Personal Is Political." Every debate in this book—from how men and women talk to each other to the pay gap to pornography to the new fatherhood to the division of housework—exists in the mainstream of discourse not as a discussion of radically complex and novel aspects of human interaction, but as lament on supposedly obvious facts. "How can this still be happening?" "Why won't society change?" "Why won't the world treat me better?" Under examination, the situation is always more chaotic; nothing is obvious when it comes to the state of men and women in the twenty-first century.

Instead of furious despair, what our moment demands is humility and compassion. Men and women living together as equals is not easy; it reveals new asymmetries rather than destroys old ones. We're in a new order we barely understand: everyone is going to fuck up, and probably most of the time. The approach to equality is filled with turbulence, not equilibrium. For the immediate future, it promises an overflowing embarrassment. And the turbulence and embarrassment will be worked out in our everyday lives, in strip clubs and in playgrounds and in offices, through the changes in our lifestyles (ancient word). We must ride the turbulence or perish.

In the game of identity politics the stakes are the righteousness of the players. One need only demonstrate, with as much conviction as possible, that one is on the right side of history. Loudness is important. The louder the outrage, the better. Argument drifts into irrelevance. The old boys' networks love it. You want Jane Austen on the ten-pound note? Done. (It will keep the newspapers from discussing why there has never been a female chancellor of the exchequer in British history.) The kamikaze leaders of progressivism have been inherently self-defeating, but they hardly mind. The point is to lose with grace. The point is to nurture the idea of oneself as a victim, while doing so from what is self-evidently a position of privilege— since these debates occur overwhelmingly on campuses or on websites filled with posts by Ivy League graduates or in the op-ed pages of major newspapers. Naturally the pursuit of victim status does nothing to help victims; it indulges tortured intellectual absurdities instead.

Under the faceless barrage of loathing that the Internet unleashes, the organic response is to join in or to run and hide, to root out the failures of your allies, to pursue ideological safety as a replacement for physical safety. But the business of correcting idealism is a parlor game in which, one by one, everybody leaves the room. Empty rooms are boring, and besides, they're empty. Personal politics has become a kind of hygiene of history, and living with others is messy, often filthy. We have brushed the dirt of centuries from our bodies. Do we have the courage to sink our hands into the muck again? An intimate gender politics will not be pure.

Outrage and the pursuit of correctness are modes of purity. The intellectual poses of a vacuous correctness are attractive exactly because they make such good cover. The culture of outrage is so popular because it's so convenient, so efficient. And undemanding too: it requires no empathy, no study. Merely apply the simplistic principles of the new virtue more loudly than your neighbor. When those simplistic principles fail, when the world fails to improve, lapse into despair. Despair has no responsibilities. The consequences of the toxic environment of current gender debates could not be more severe. It has become morally dangerous to discuss the ideas that are the most complex and the most important to our shared lives. You don't just risk making an intellectual mistake; you risk revealing yourself as a terrible person. The screamers have raised the stakes to the point where data and exchange have a highly circumscribed and limited place.

The problem with identity politics is not the politics part; it's the identity part. Identity politics strips identity of its danger and unfathomability and fits it into handy social categories. The shallow poses conform to only the crudest facts of identity, unconcerned with the unfathomable depths of its various origins and the intense flux of the transformation we are undergoing. Rather than enrich the realm of politics with the difficult business of intimate life, identity politics flattens the personal until it fits into established intellectual categories. What gets lost is the tormented, gorgeous, infuriating, labyrinthine space between power and intimacy, where the substance of the human drama lives, and the mystery of love. It's in this space that we live. And only in this space can we hope to find out what men and women might be.

SIX

—

The Boys' Crisis, the Girls' Crisis

THE most dramatic scenes have the most banal settings. My wife and I perched on the tiny, uncomfortable chairs in my son's kindergarten, a room smelling faintly of markers and boredom, and across from us his awkwardly smiling teacher, a lovely young woman who cared deeply for his well-being, her hands delicately folded on her lap, gave us the news as gently as possible, which made it even more chilling. "Your boy is a bit of a mess."

Is this the beginning? My instinctive thought. Is this the first of a hundred conversations with a hundred teachers, each smiling, each with her hands folded delicately on her lap? Is this the first of a hundred bland rooms smelling of markers and boredom? Is this the original of many messes to come? My son's teacher was referring, literally, to his unkempt hair and his backpack full of crumpled paper and his indecipherable handwriting, but I knew she was also speaking to a vaguer, more indefinable sense of messiness, the messiness I also carry around in myself—his disorganization, the way he throws his body around, the condition sometimes known, with a comical lightening to mask the throat-constricting judgment, as the "wigglybums" but is more usually identified, with lowered voice, as Difficulty Concentrating.

It's not like Sarah and I hadn't been expecting it. When my wife and I sat across from my son's teacher, all three of us knew that the condition we were dealing with was not solely about him but was also about his gender. The hollow patriarchy—the rise of women to dominance of the middle, with men at either extreme—has left boys in a hole. As my wife and I sat down to deal with the messiness of our son, we knew the stakes were high but also that we were not alone. Far from it. Our problem was typical: the problem with boys.

* * *

Children are delicacies of fear that comes in two flavors: boy and girl. I've tasted both varieties. A family friend—an old-school feminist, the kind with the Rosie the Riveter "We Can Do It!" poster in the bathroom, photos from Zionist summer camps in the hallway, and many brightly patterned, shapeless tunics in her closet—once told me, "If you have a daughter, you worry about the rapists. If you have a son, you worry that he will become the rapist." That's broadly fair, it seems to me. When I hold my daughter, I fear the world. Step outside the little bubble of Western democracy, and the notion of the boys' crisis verges on the obscenely hilarious. A girl growing up poor in sub-Saharan Africa has a less than one-in-four chance of going to school. In the rich West antique misogynies lurk everywhere. What I fear for my daughter is that the world, in one guise or another, in the figure of a monster or a man or other women or a cloud of oppressive expectation, will one day step into her life and crush her dreams, subtly or violently, invidiously or outright, with the proverbial but also literal whimper or bang.* The girls' crisis is ubiquitous and ancient. The boys' crisis is local and new.

The reality of the souls of children, and the confusing business of being responsible for them, is where the theoretical constructs of gender and the messiness of life meet and where

---

*As a Jewish mother, my catalogue of worries about my kids is comically long. I worry about water seeping into winter boots, about snacks being crushed in backpacks, about the mild eczema that both my kids have. I worry a lot about them being hit by cars. I also share Steve's worries about boys in the modern classroom, but less so. A few weeks ago I attended the parent visit day at my son's fourth grade Jewish Sunday school. The classroom configuration: About seven tidy girls sat in the front row, books neatly organized on their desks, eyes facing the blackboard, each girl eagerly awaiting an opportunity to please the teacher. There were only four boys in the class because each year since preschool one or two boys had dropped out of the program. The boys were in the second row, giggling over a silly cartoon one of them had drawn, utterly uninterested in the lesson. I worry that the boys are being left behind. On the other hand, that rebellious, freethinking kid who drew the cartoon will probably go on to have an interesting, innovative career that will reward him financially for thinking creatively.

the impositions of our antique traditions, often invisible to ourselves, meet our hopes for the future. In the revolution of intimacy children are the ultimate theater of conflict. Children reveal the poverty of our thinking, the ludicrousness of our assumptions, the uselessness of our most coveted beliefs. And exactly in the face of what is most precious to us, exactly at the moment we crave certainty.

It has now been more than a decade since Christina Hoff Sommers wrote her landmark bestseller, *The War Against Boys*. A cry of anger, a lamentation from the heart, and a thoroughly researched assault on the entire system of pedagogy, *The War Against Boys* sparked massive public debate. Boys have not lacked for articulate defenders since—dozens of titles have followed—but the fate of boys has only darkened. The boys' crisis is accelerating ferociously. ADHD diagnosis increased by 3 percent a year from 1997 to 2003 and 5 percent a year from 2003 to 2011. Boys get 70 percent of Ds and Fs in school. The typical eleventh grade boy writes at the same level as an eighth grade girl. Boys are expelled from primary school five times as often as girls. Boys' delinquency rate is three times what it is for girls. Boys account for two-thirds of school suspensions.

The educational divergence between men and women, which was alarming before the recession of 2008, has swollen into science fiction territory since. Women now account for nearly 60 percent of all university enrollments. By the time my son is in college, in all likelihood, 66 percent of all educated people will be women. What will it be like when the category *man* is synonymous with the category *uneducated,* which will be synonymous with the category *failure?*

The time of warning has passed. The results are in: worse education leads to worse employment outcomes. The traditionally male fields are in decline or are highly vulnerable to recession, and women dominate thirteen of the fifteen largest growth fields. And all of it leads to a dramatic spike in despair, as evidenced by the dramatic spike in male suicide rates. You don't have to read the statistics. The world is filling up with lost boys; you can see them if you care to look. They hang out in the parking lots of small towns. They squat on corners or under bridges in big cities. They drift in the hills, warming themselves on fires that sometimes spread out of control. They are threatening insofar as they are purposeless. Their danger is in proportion to their uselessness.

The boys' crisis is morphing into a men's crisis.

* * *

Sarah remembers pushing our toddler son in a grocery cart while he entertained himself with a banana pointed like a gun, shooting a procession of bad guys as they emerged from behind the vegetable aisle. A female shopper winced as they passed. "They're all like that, aren't they?" she said. "All like what?" Sarah wanted to ask, but didn't because she's Canadian. They're all natural-born killers? Or they all want to play with fruit?

Boys have not changed much over the past two decades. But the reaction to them has. The instinct to negate them has triumphed. Even the literature on the boys' crisis has generated a self-feeding loop; the plea for boys turns inevitably to warning.

Fear is the first response, rife even among their defenders, and after the fear comes the blame, two brands of it: right-wing and left-wing. At the beginning of the debate *The War Against Boys* was explicitly a critique of feminism. Boys were the new girls, limited and despised by a generalized misandry, a politically correct fury that, in its zeal to tear down the patriarchy, simply forgot that men are people. The sociologist Michael Kimmel, a leading theorist of masculinity, has offered the other perspective, first in his 2008 book, *Guyland*, and again in 2013's *Angry White Men*. Kimmel argues that the residue of patriarchy drives young men to despair and self-destruction. The old codes, the macho, the defensive response to a changing world, "the ideology of traditional masculinity that keeps boys from wanting to succeed" are the primary culprits.

Neither approach is satisfying when you actually have a kid you're trying to deal with. "Traditional masculinity," as I have understood it my entire life, and indeed as I see it for most of human history, involves wanting to succeed at school, and at everything else for that matter. On the other hand, the idea that boys face some kind of serious reverse discrimination is deluded. Fitting boys into an inverted victimology inherited from an outmoded gender war isn't helpful. If there is a war on boys, who is the army arrayed against them? Was my son's teacher the enemy? She certainly didn't think so, and neither do I. She wanted the best for my boy, without a doubt. She just wanted less mess. She wanted quiet. The problem was that she had no idea how to deal with the boyishness except to contain it, to wish it away.

Not that I had any better ideas, at least not at first. After the conversation with his teacher I had a good look at my son and the boys around him. There are problem boys in this world. There are boys with attention-deficit disorders and anxiety disorders, boys who genuinely need medication. There are boys with autism and boys who are plain devils. My boy is not one of them. My boy is a typical boy. He's the boy Tom Waits was thinking of when he wrote about the little boys who never comb their hair. I was this same boy.

My son never combs his hair. He runs in, smelling of mud and rain, and throws his jacket and shoes on the floor as he rushes upstairs to find the page in a book of the world's most dangerous animals that he has been thinking about all day, to see which is deadlier: the anaconda or the black mamba. He doesn't want to sit. He doesn't want to do crafts. He wants to walk in the light forests with their dark margins. He wants to talk to his friends about movies. He wants to play video games and wrestle on the beach. In short, he's a boy—physical, tribal, tender, restless, testing his limits. When I looked at my son's school, at his life, I saw a basic failure even to recognize that his boyish nature existed. (And yes, the black mamba is deadlier, by far.)

* * *

The distinction between the nature of boys and the nature of girls could not be more clear or more vague. It is tied to an ultimately intractable conundrum: How different are men and women? Are we men and women first, or are we people who happen to be men and women? Do we belong to different species, or do we have different decorations? Are boys and girls distinct in their essences or only by accident of birth? These are questions to which the answers may be unknowable.

Even the Bible doesn't have an answer, or rather it has two conflicting answers. In Genesis 1:27 God makes Adam and Eve together, simultaneously, in the image of himself: "Male and female created he them." In 2:18 Eve is explicitly created as an addendum, a "help meet" made from Adam's rib for his service. So are men and women both created in the image of God, or only men? Obviously an emphasis on either of these two passages produces distinct visions of the nature of humanity, and a whole array of contradictory political and aesthetic consequences follow.

You don't have to read Genesis to be confused. Scientific approaches to the nature of gender distinction have replicated the duality, rephrasing the question rather than answering it. In 2013 a data analyst and a professor of psychology, Bobbi Carothers and Harry Reis, applied mathematical modeling to the question of the difference between men and women. They undertook a large metastudy, a study of all the other studies on gender differences, and established which were "taxonic," meaning nonarbitrary biological categories, and which were "dimensional," showing qualitative differences along a spectrum. Applying these competing models to a huge array of issues, including virtually every kind of psychological indicator and personality trait, sexual attitudes, the capacity for empathy, levels of intimacy with friends and family, even physical strength, led to the same conclusion: "In all instances the dimensional approach prevailed." Differences between men and women are not essential but exist along a spectrum.

All is a very big number. It almost amounts to a conclusion. "Gender differences *on average* are not under dispute," Carothers and Reis acknowledge. "The idea of consistently and inflexibly gender-typed individuals is. That is, there are not two distinct genders, but instead there are linear gradations of variables associated with sex." The purely biological differences between men and women are negligible, or at least are much smaller than we might have thought. The title of Carothers and Reis's paper? "Men and Women Are from Earth."

Six months after the release of "Men and Women Are from Earth" an extensive study of the brain scans of 949 male and female youths came to the opposite conclusion: "The results establish that male brains are optimized for intrahemispheric and female brains for interhemispheric communication. The developmental trajectories of males and females separate at a young age, demonstrating wide differences during adolescence and adulthood." The way the brain signals across sides is different for men and women.

To summarize: the latest evidence, from the best sources, establishes that we are more or less the same but also completely and utterly different. The answers to the question of gender difference are as unsatisfying as they have ever been. Archaic religion and the latest science has to offer are equally baffling. Gender theory is no more helpful than either, reflecting the same impossible duality. Judith Butler famously argued that gender is a "cultural fiction" or, in the pseudo-philosophical language that infected academia in her time, "performative in the sense that the essence or identity that they otherwise purport to express are fabrications manufactured and sustained through corporeal signs." Later Butler attempted to clarify, claiming that "the reduction of performativity to performance would be a mistake." But the contradiction remains in force, undermining the whole project of gender studies. Gender is both a performance and not. This is knowledge, but it is not the kind of knowledge that helps.

Total theoretical incoherence is not necessarily a failing; it may be intellectual honesty. Among the differences between men and women there are biological realities; there are performances of gender; there are performances repeated so often that they feel like biological realities. Separating these distinctions is not always possible. Gender, as a concept, is inherently elusive. If somebody tells you there is no biological difference between men and women, he is wrong. If somebody else tells you she knows what the nature of that difference is, she too is wrong.

* * *

As we approach equality, the nature of gender does not become clearer. Rather the opposite. How we live gender and how we think about it are divided across a chasm. We may believe that the differences between men and women are elusive, but we cannot act as if they are. That trickiness confronts anyone trying to educate boys and girls.

In the 1990s Butler's ideas, or rather a crude version of

them, bled down into the substrata of pedagogic assumption. Hers was one of the rare academic theories to translate into widespread change. When it comes to gender, "nature" is not something anybody wants to talk about anymore. The intellectual basis for institutional equality—anything boys can do, girls can do—runs on an assumption of biological equality and gender as a performance. Simple vanity also had something to do with the triumph of those assumptions. The dominance of nurture elevates teachers' social status; they become capable of correcting historical injustices, weeding out antiquated prejudices, and altering the world by using its most malleable and powerful change agents: young minds. If the inequities of gender are primarily cultural, then the solution is to impose a different culture. Teachers therefore become trench warriors because boys and girls have to be treated the same in school in order that men and women will be treated the same in society at large. Equality is sameness. Sameness is fairness.

Children are the repositories of our utopian hopes about gender, as about many things. A couple in Toronto achieved a kind of semifame by rendering their utopianism explicit: they are raising one of their children without gender. Storm's gender is known only to them and a few select friends. "A tribute to freedom and choice in place of limitation, a stand up to what the world could become in Storm's lifetime (a more progressive place?)," the parents posted on Facebook. Storm's parents seem sweet, living off the grid northeast of Parry Sound, Ontario, worrying about the media circus they inevitably caused, recording what Storm likes and dislikes, sharing their doubts about Storm's inability to consent to be non-gender-assigned. I try never to judge parents who are loving, as Storm's parents obviously are. Children are entitled to love in their upbringing, not intelligence. Nonetheless gender refusal—or, to put it another way, the refusal to gender-diagnose—seems to me to be the height of folly. Rather than remove gender from Storm's life, they have made it the whole subject of his or her existence. Storm was a monster for Halloween, the parents posted. Is that something boys do, or girls?

Storm's gender-neutralizing is an extension of standard parental folly. His or her parents imagine that by changing the name, they will change the child. At age two my son became obsessed with heavy machinery, with the distinctions between a front-end loader and a dump truck, between a semi and an eighteen-wheeler. He did so with exactly zero male modeling. I know nothing about cars or trucks or construction; my father had a PhD in semantics, and my father-in-law is a highly uncoordinated newspaper columnist. No man in my son's life could have told him how a front-end loader works. No man in his life had ever owned a truck. Nonetheless the boy played with front-end loaders and trucks. My daughter, at the age of eighteen months, started playing with dolls, even though there was an equally prevalent absence of female modeling for her. One day she was in a shoe store and simply grabbed a doll off the shelf. Now she needs to put the doll to bed before she will go to sleep.

These choices were theirs, I believe. At least I know they weren't mine. I follow in the slipstreams of their behavior, as I believe most parents do.* And I'm not sure that the choices I took to be gendered were anywhere near the most important. At one point my daughter fell in love with her soiled diapers and wouldn't let us throw them out. There was also a time when she liked to lead her friends out of the schoolyard on wild adventures just beyond whatever fence she was explicitly told not to pass. At three she sometimes likes to jump up and down on my chest, smashing her heels into me, to see if she can knock the wind out of me. She stares into my eyes to see if she's hurting me. My son used to take off his clothes while we were visiting museums and run away from us, naked, for a laugh. This isn't gender weirdness. It's kid weirdness. It's person weirdness.

One of the stranger fantasies of our moment—a necessary illusion perhaps—is that we are in control of who our children are, what they become, and what they mean. This is one of those widespread notions that we accept even though it contradicts all evidence and common sense, like the bizarre idea that people are supposed to be happy—a nearly ubiquitous belief that finds

---

*Like many women my age who attended college in the 1990s, when academic feminism was in vogue, I emerged into adulthood convinced that gender was overwhelmingly a cultural construct. Then I had kids. What a humbling business it is to watch all your beliefs crumble in the hands of a pair of toddlers. My daughter likes to organize the shoes in the front hall. My son takes his off while bounding into the house, scattering sand from the playground, obliviously. I'm trying to teach my son to pick his socks up from the floor so that his future partner doesn't have to date a guy who leaves his laundry lying around.

no support in the medical or historical records.

Children are people, a fact that eludes almost all discussion. They possess the fundamental mystery of their particularity—the mystery that lies at the root of human dignity. Occasionally my three-year-old daughter will insist that I shave. She will stand at the top of the stairs and shout, "Daddy shave, Daddy shave, Daddy shave." And I inevitably do shave. She's always right anyway; I do need a shave when she screams for it. What does this mean? That she will grow up to be a hairdresser? That she will grow up to be bossy? That I have shaped her relationship to facial hair forever? No doubt I am changing my daughter. But who can say how? I remember my son drinking his first sip of soda water. He considered it. "This water's sunburned," he said. (I later purloined this line for a short story.) Where could such a phrase, *sunburned water*, have come from? The expected surprise and the unbearable exhilaration of growth are the substance of lived temporality. Hold on to your children because you cannot hold on to them: they will never be exactly like this again.

*   *   *

The desire to erase gender distinction is a simple, logical extension of the desire for gender equality on all terms. But the approach to equality, which is at bottom an attempt to treat men and women as fully human, settles eventually into an unsatisfying lack of clarity. In a patriarchal society in which children are raised in patriarchal schools by patriarchal parents, one could simply assume that the difference between boys and girls is the inevitable result of the educational system. But gender distinctions between children still emerge even when those patriarchal ideas are ruthlessly rooted out.

The day care my son attended in Toronto was scrupulously politically correct. How politically correct? One day government inspectors came by to see that all the regulations were being fulfilled, and they found two infringements: that there weren't enough dolls of color available to the children and that there weren't enough positive images of people with disabilities. The day care could have been shut down for either. So the next morning, before any children showed up, a huge picture of an African-American kid in a wheelchair playing tennis was hung over the front door. Even in an institution so scrupulous about the political acceptability of the representations it permitted, the first day I dropped my son off I noticed all the little girls sitting at a table dressing dolls while the little boys were running around the table, kicking each other, having folded the dolls into the shape of guns.*

Difference has a tendency to assert itself, despite what we

---

*I visited five or six day cares in Brooklyn. They were almost all in fluorescent-lit repurposed storefronts, with cheap carpets and a pervasive smell of bleach. They were all unregulated. The owners were entrepreneurial women who I suspected were just as concerned with cost management as they were with baby care. Canada requires day care staff to hold early childhood education degrees. The one our son went to when we first moved back had unionized staff. The government inspects them regularly. They are often the first choice of upper-middle-class educated parents. None of my American friends can fathom any of this.

might wish. There is solid evidence that gender separation in schools helps both boys and girls. A 2013 study conducted in Korea, which admits children to coed or single-sex schools randomly (removing self-selection bias), came to the conclusion that "attending all-boys schools or all-girls schools, rather than attending coeducational schools, is significantly associated with higher average scores on Korean and English test scores." Educators have known for generations that boys and girls need different things to be successful in the classroom. The differences in need can be broad—boys need more structure— but they can also be surprisingly elemental; for instance, boys do better in cooler rooms, and girls do better in warmer rooms. The boys' crisis is another example of the old lesson *Nature asserts itself. Always.* The conscious effort of so many individuals and institutions to impose equality between boys and girls has revealed the reality of gender difference by contrast.

Thrown out the door for criminal behavior, gender distinction returns like the prodigal son, to be feasted, its reputation somewhat restored. The prodigal return of difference cuts to the most sensitive spot in our lives: the kids. The son of two moms who turns into the hockey jock. The daughter of the feminist professor of the sociology of gender who won't leave the house unless dressed completely in pink. We've all seen it. And the research confirms the anecdotes. Studies from as early as the 1970s found that boys prefer trucks and girls prefer dolls. For many years it was assumed that the difference between boys and girls was simply the product of deep-seated cultural mechanisms. In 2002, however, two evolutionary psychologists,

Gerianne Alexander and Melissa Hines, noticed a significant exception to the gender division in playtime. A genetic disorder occasionally led to higher levels of androgen in the womb than normal, and mothers who were prescribed hormone treatments during pregnancy showed the same increases. The daughters of these mothers overwhelmingly preferred to play with boys and with their toys. Did socialization therefore not have as profound an effect on toy selection as previously believed? What if the differences in play couldn't be explained by the assumptions placed on children? What if the explanation was simpler, deeper?

Alexander and Hines decided to look beyond the merely human. At the UCLA/Sepulveda Veterans Administration Nonhuman Primate Laboratory they offered eighty-eight vervet monkeys living in seven different social groups a set of six toys: a ball, a police car, a doll, a cooking pot, a picture book, and a stuffed dog. The ball and the police car were categorized as "masculine," the pot and doll were "feminine," and the book and stuffed dog were neutral. They found that both male and female monkeys approached all the toys, but male monkeys played more with the boy toys and girl monkeys played more with the girl toys. A similar test in 2008 using rhesus monkeys further supported Alexander and Hines's theory that the gender distinction in human modes of play evolved on the primate level. Since the 1970s, as gender roles in the culture at large have expanded, children's toys have become more gendered and more traditional. Every boy a truck driver and every girl a princess. The Disney Store has a boys' page and a girls' page on its website.

This distinction in styles of play and toy preferences may seem only a curiosity, but its consequences are profound, because style of play leads to the development of gender identities, both cognitively and socially. Boys play with boys and girls play with girls, and the split is evidence not of a symptom but of a cause of difference. Play is the beginning of work. Play is more serious than work, because play is the underlying meaning of all that work can be. A child in the rapture of deep play should never be interrupted. Playing children re-create, with each game, that terrible seismic moment, whose consequences remain to be worked out, when mammals began to shape the world. Every little girl who organizes a tea party is rebuilding, from scratch, the whole of civil society. Every boy who builds a backyard fort remakes all of Rome. Adults laugh at the self-styled seriousness of infant efforts, the tender concentration of little fingers investigating the line between immanence and transcendence. They should remember that all human efforts are laughable.

* * *

What I saw in my own boy was that his boyishness had to have an outlet and that I would have to find him one. Parenting advice today has become like dieting advice in the 1980s: many schemes are promoted; many schemes are debunked. But to be a parent is necessarily to be a bumbler; nobody really knows what they're talking about. That's why having kids is humbling and maturing; you realize that, about the important things in life, we're all stumbling around in the dark, taking hope where we can find it.

The main experience of parenthood is exhaustion and filth and being responsible for vastly complex and vulnerable organisms. There is little room for originality or innovation. When you are holding a shitty diaper, you throw it in the closest receptacle. When your daughter can't fall asleep, you sing the old songs, the tunes that you know have worked to put other babies to sleep over the centuries.

After much bumbling I found various ways for my son to express his inner boyishness: martial arts, team sports, rock climbing, summer camp. Embarrassing clichés, but they worked. My son had no problem standing still in a gym when ordered to by a coach. He had no difficulty with concentration when he was dangling from a rope fifteen feet up a climbing wall. He was not disruptive singing songs around a campfire. Watching him flourish in these activities was like releasing a bird into the air and watching it fly. Oh, so this is where you were supposed to be all the time. It was also oddly disappointing. These are the best solutions I could find? The old solutions?

Here was the position I found myself in: I had to reckon with my son's masculine nature within an egalitarian system. I wanted to preserve both. Or rather I sensed that my son needed both: belonging to groups that encouraged his nature while having the freedom to become whatever he chose. What I wanted was an approach that retained the best features of the traditional ways of teaching boys while not indulging the old restricted visions or fantasizing some hollow vision of deliberately stupid masculinity. A related problem, equally difficult to solve, is how to be a proud man without being an asshole about it.

These are questions every man and every parent of a son face. Unfortunately they demand intelligence, which is not a requirement for becoming either a man or a parent. They involve thoughtfully and consciously selecting the values we want from the past without buying into the supposed male supremacy those values emerged from. They involve the search for equality while accepting the realities of difference. Call it neotraditionalism, or even neopatriarchy. Or call it modern fatherhood: the struggle to retain respect for the nature of boys, and of men, without patriarchy's treatment of women as subhuman and the narrow confines of antique identities.

One thing is becoming certain: to forget gender difference, either by accident or intentionally, is disastrous for boys. It is no coincidence that the boys' crisis arose at the same moment as the crisis of fatherlessness, with the disappearance of the male example. Exposure to exemplars of masculinity are so necessary for boys because, in their absence, the most simplistic ideas of manhood triumph. The iconoclasm of male heroes has stranded men in their attempts at self-articulation. One by one the patriarchs have been deposed or have deposed themselves. The priests turned out to be diddlers, the coaches savage bullies. The past fifty years have been consumed with the destruction of various patriarchies, and they deserved to be destroyed. But the coaches and priests are not the enemies of civil society; they are its creators. Without them, things fall apart. The crisis has been caused by men removing themselves, absenting themselves, checking out, not giving a shit about anyone but themselves.

To know a real-life man is to know that the ideals of traditional masculinity are, at most, conditional fantasies. Sports remains the great teaching ground for boys because, even though the focus is on winning, the lessons are mostly about losing. You try to win, but you live with loss—the fundamental lesson of all competitive children's activities. When my father died, two lines kept running through my head, one from *Hamlet* and the other from the baseball movie *Bull Durham*. When told that his father was a good king, Hamlet replies only, "He was a man, take him for all in all." In *Bull Durham*, when the hot pitcher Nuke LaLoosh is pitching poorly because his father is videotaping him, his catcher Crash Davis tells him, "He's just your old man. He's as full of shit as anybody." The insight is the same in both: actual patriarchs have the vulnerabilities inherent in masculinity. The ghettos and the prisons are full of tough guys who think that being a man is never showing any weakness. They are the brittle men, whose shattering is so dangerous.

Sommers and Kimmel are both right: the men lost without a patriarchy and the men lost in guyland *are the same men*. What has been taken away from boys are the visions of manhood as much as the entitlements of patriarchy, and without those visions, the boys lack the frames within which to develop the emotional complexity required to be fully fledged men. The bridge over the chasm between boyhood and manhood has two parallel spans: give boys and men a way to be proud to be men in order that they can then understand that being a man is an ongoing, difficult, complicated undertaking that involves failing a great deal. It's not that the boys' crisis requires a complex response. Complexity *is* the response. Nuance is the path to salvation.

There is a war today between two types of men: those who are so threatened that their masculinity emerges only in vacuous macho and those who are confident enough to recognize that emotional complexity is part of every man's life. We have a choice of confusions. We must make sure we choose the right one.

* * *

The problem is that complexity and nuance are anathema to massive institutions like, say, the Department of Education. The first nuance to be negotiated, and the most fraught, is how we distinguish girls and boys.

Unfortunately a cultural shift toward recognition of boys' needs seems a long way off. The boy is now an alien among us, brittle but also violent, to be feared or pitied or both. But you don't have to look far back to find other responses. Not so long ago boys and boyishness were ideals. On the walls of the American Museum of Natural History in Manhattan are written the hopes Teddy Roosevelt had for the boys of his era: "I want to see you game, boys, I want to see you brave and manly, and I also want to see you gentle and tender." Boys used to be strong but also sentimental; the camaraderie of young men was the basis of larger social belonging, the source of the desire to contribute to a power greater than oneself, the model of community itself. For most of the twentieth century boys represented the best of humanity. Our expectation of boys has shifted from "Go out and do great things" to "Sit still and be quiet." The biology of boys is not destroying them; the culture is, and culture can be changed. Boyhood and manhood will have to be revised together.

Love of children and fear of the world arrive in stutter-step tandem. Cortisol dances with oxytocin from the beginning. Right after the rush of birth, the very next act is to fit the baby into a car safety seat. Here is new life: don't wreck it. The anxieties are interwoven with our hopes. Not the least of the pleasurable horrors and abject joys of parenting is the forced reckoning with the unpredictability of the future, the wildness of life. What will become of them, my big-hearted boy, curious and tender; my daughter, who is so trusting she will take the hands of strangers in crowds to be led into dimly sensed, half-promised adventures. Your heart is out walking around in the world. How much do you trust the world? How much do you trust your own heart?

A world filled with lost boys, with boys torn apart by phony masculinity, tossed by shallow dreams of what their desires should be and what the world expects of them, is a world filled with girls who will eventually have to live with these boys. For both girls and boys we want the same thing. We want them to escape the snares of being told what they are, and we also want them to flourish in their nature. We want for our children the chance to be fully human in all the impossibility that entails.

* * *

I remain worried about my son. He runs when he should not run. He shouts when he should not shout. When he walks in the street, his conception of the personal space of others is vague at best. Parenthood is a low thrum of anxiety, relieved by staccato bursts of joy and panic. To be a parent is to be worried. It's not supposed to be any other way.

The year after our first conversation with his teacher, my wife and I found ourselves sitting on another pair of uncomfortable chairs in another bland room smelling of markers and anxiety. This time we brought up the boy's messiness first, knowing it was coming. His new teacher shrugged. "He's a boy," she said, as if it were the most obvious thing in the world. Her shrug of acknowledgment was worth more than any advice she could offer. It showed that boys are not given to the world as problems to be solved, by the use of algorithm or sociological experiment. Boys and girls are here to be loved.

SEVEN

The Case for Living in Filth

M EANWHILE there's housework. Sex is beautiful and dangerous, babies are born, fathers die, children are worries, but the housework is waiting always. A house is work. One goes with the other.

It's strictly a question of perspective: Do my wife and I own a house, or are we swallowed every night into the hungry belly of a stationary, numbered beast? Our house-beast is cozy and squat, more than a century old. It has "good bones," so I have been told, as if the roof beams over the dining room were thick ribs, and when I held the thrill-seeking babies up to grab them, the house was being tickled from the inside.

The house has its own orders, its own exchange of airs and energies, just like a body. I am writing this in the attic, where I am kept behind a door that locks both ways with the books and records and other curios. Below me are the bedrooms on the second floor, where the pools of the family's identities lap against each other—my son's walls postered with One

Direction and Harry Potter and SpongeBob SquarePants; my daughter's room, shared with her communion of dolls, who stare at each other with their half-lidded eyes; our bedroom, a bare room with no art but a cello sitting like a plump aunt in the corner. I think we haven't decorated the bedroom because we are both so tired of making decisions. On the ground floor the gumwood-paneled living and dining rooms, classically Edwardian in their cozy melancholy, serve mainly as an extended indoor climbing gym, strewn with toys that have been picked up and put down, books that have been picked up and put down. The blinds on the front window had to be removed; my son broke too many slats leaping over the sofa, fleeing from bad guys of his imagination. The kitchen is the heart, like the stitched platitude says, humming with refrigerated food and leaking taps.

As in many bodies, the dark corners of the house are the most tender. In the kitchen a cup of red wine vinegar covered with Saran wrap pocked with holes traps fruit flies. The basement holds the detritus of previous lives: letters from ex-girlfriends and ex-boyfriends, a garden hose coiled in futility, the summer tires of a car I crashed, boxes of Christmas decorations, a wall of CDs long since transferred to digital, the toys no longer desired, the empty bottles waiting to be taken back for deposit, a claw-foot bathtub kept in a small chamber once used to store coal. A previous owner must have found a way to bring down that bathtub; it will stay there until a future owner figures out a way to bring it up.

Sarah and I are only temporary acolytes of this redbrick idol.

Others came before us. Others will come after us. The house-beast needs to have its various vanities assuaged with regular sacrifices, nightly sweeping and washing of its surfaces, and the shaving of its front lawn so that it won't be embarrassed in front of the neighbors. It requires the biweekly sacrifice of huge piles of money to an Australian mortgage company, along with other irregular whimsical expenses, roofs and boilers and many, many surprises. Every now and then it needs to be told it's loved, so we paint the walls or clean the windows. As in any symbiosis, general affection is offset by intermittent resentment. All this trouble for shelter. But how could it be any other way? The trouble is the price of intimacy. Housework is intimate trouble.

* * *

At the end of all comedy, housework is waiting, right after sex. "Reader, I married him" is how *Jane Eyre* ends. No epilogue explains the specific breakdown of duties and responsibilities established in the subsequent domestic arrangement. *Eat, Pray, Love* stopped at "Love." There was no fourth part titled "Chores," because it would have taken too long and nobody would have read it.

Sex inevitably progresses indoors. Sex begins in stolen spaces: the backs of cars, parks, basement couches. Sex continues through a phase of "your place or mine"—the tragicomic negotiations of apartments and hotels, which is why sex farces on stage inevitably involve the closing and opening of many doors. Moving in together is the real decision between lovers. Moving in together means you have to consider the reality of another person, not now and then but all the time, over the course of the entire day, every day. In contemporary romantic life housework and children are the true gauges of intimacy; sex is a lark, and marriage is paperwork. When a man and a woman fall into bed together, they might have each other; when one of them makes the bed, they have a relationship.

At the moment I could leave my computer and tidy the stairs to my office, replace the back gate's slat that was lost during a recent storm, clean the lunch dishes. I could paint the ceiling in the bedroom, which grew slightly dampstained after a snow-packed winter. I could go into the garden, where I really should trim the hedges and hack back the grapevines on the trellis. I'm not even thinking about treating the deck, which will take half a week at least. But I won't do any of them, at least not now. Even the fact that I will have to do them at some point is oppressive. Housework is a fundamental dreariness between human beings,* a dreariness that necessarily consumes far more

---

*Not everyone feels that way. Tidying up a house can be satisfying. Creating a warm home can be an act of love. Of course, chores are boring, but housework is like most work: the act of doing it isn't so pleasurable; you do it for the results. A clean house is nice. It is relaxing. Being in a well-run, ordered environment feels good. Housework is something to be endured if you want that feeling badly enough. Steve usually doesn't crave a clean house as much as he craves all the other things he'd rather do—like watch the baseball game, or write an essay, or read a story to our toddler. When I enter a messy space my gut desire to declutter it is utterly overwhelming. A friend of mine who lives nearby has a really messy house. She's got a big career and a big brain and a big heart and she does a lot of good in the world. She doesn't care that her house is messy. My reaction to her house is one

time and effort and emotion than joy. A house, no matter how much love it contains, is a collection of unpleasant tasks and tender gestures, duties and expectations, disgusting tasks and half-noticed considerations.

It's also the sphere of life where the question of gender equality is not statistics but everyday action, not theoretical abstraction but nitty-gritty. There are worse definitions of power than the difference between those who clean up and those who don't.

* * *

Housework equality is in a state of stasis. In 1989 Arlie Hochschild published her highly influential study of working parents, *The Second Shift*. After studying the wild discrepancies between what household responsibilities couples thought they shared and what they actually shared, she concluded that women who worked out of the house were no less exempt from the traditional role of homemaker than women who didn't. In the 1980s America became a nation of supermoms—doctors going home to vacuum before the dinner party, partner-track lawyers cooking all weekend to fill the basement freezer, and so

---

of great conflict; I vaguely disapprove and quietly wonder how she can stand it, while at the same time I admire her ability not to care. I also know I shouldn't care, but no matter how successful my generation of women are in the workforce we still judge each other's domestic spaces. My mom is neat, and I confess that I sometimes see a room through her eyes, with the value she places on an ordered space. Will my daughter see space through mine? Do I want her to?

on—doing a range and quantity of tasks that seemed not just unfair but preposterous and unsustainable. For Hochschild the discrepancy in expectations between men and women at home meant that feminism itself amounted to a "stalled revolution."

Since 1989 the realities of our sexual and financial lives have changed utterly, reconfiguring society beyond recognition. Except for housework. Cleaning up remains, against all logic and other trends, principally women's work. So it should be no surprise that the domestic realm is where the most intractable discrepancies between men and women remain; it's where the daily struggle otherwise known as the gender wars continues unabated; and it's where that struggle will have to be resolved. The crisis has been brewing for thirty years. In all that time domestic culture has not caught up with working reality. One of them will have to change.

The nub of the problem is that men will not do more housework. In the vast majority of countries in the developed world, men's time investment in housework has not significantly altered since the mid-1980s.* The largest cross-national

---

*Steve has the ability to do the most incredible thing: in the middle of domestic chaos he can block it all out and focus on something important to him. He can write a novel on his laptop while a singing toddler is building a giant Lego tower on the floor and two nine-year-old boys are jumping through the house with plastic swords and the dishes are piled up in the sink and dinner needs to be on the table in half an hour. All he sees is his work. He can do this with leisure time too: if he wants to watch a baseball game, he won't notice that the garbage needs to be taken out and the contents of the kids' backpacks

metastudy on the subject, from 2009, found that "in Canada, the United Kingdom and the Netherlands—all countries with data spanning the 1980s to 2000s—men's housework time has not budged significantly since the 1980s, with current levels at about 80 minutes a day." In the United States men's participation in housework "topped out" at ninety-four minutes a day in 1998, but by 2003 was down to eighty-one minutes, pretty close to the seventy-six minutes it was in the 1980s. The husbands of women who work do not do more housework, even when they stay at home. The husbands of women who earn more money than they do *less* housework.

Unlike virtually every other rubric by which you can establish the balance of power between men and women, there is no evidence of a cohort shift in housework. Women now are 40 percent of breadwinners in America, a share of the workforce that has quadrupled since 1960. Yet men have not added

are all over the floor and a piece of rotting fruit on the table is attracting fruit flies. He will lock his eyes on the baseball game and everything else will fade away. Or maybe he never even noticed the other stuff in the first place? When I see him on the couch, working or relaxing, in a house with a floor that needs to be swept, beds that need to be made, and dying flowers in the vase that need to be tossed out, I feel two things: anger and envy. Anger because, holy shit, get off your ass and clean up, and envy because it's actually pretty healthy to be able to focus on one thing instead of constantly puttering about doing triage on an endlessly demanding domestic space. It would be so nice to just plunk myself down and have that kind of focus, to be present in the moment. I honestly don't know if there's something wrong with me because I can't do it or something wrong with him because he can.

domestic responsibilities to compensate for their diminished breadwinner responsibilities. Not even a little bit.

Removing, for a moment, the question of economic fairness, men's more or less outright refusal to do more housework is also genuinely mysterious. Why won't men help around the house? Think of all the other changes that men, or most men anyway, have undertaken in the period between 1980 and 2010. Taking care of kids used to be women's work too; now the man playing with his kids is an icon of manliness. Foodie snobbism has taken on an explicitly macho edge, to the point where the properly brined Thanksgiving turkey is a stereotypical status symbol of male achievement. So why won't men pick up a broom? Why won't they organize a closet? Why can't housework be converted—as the former burdens of food preparation and child rearing have been—into a source of manly pride and joy? Why would housework be the place to stall?

Despite its apparent banality, housework has always been an intellectually confounding problem. Defining chores as a bunch of repetitive tasks undertaken to preserve the health and hygiene of the living space is inaccurate. Housework is as complex as the connection between our emotional life and our material life, as subtle as all intimacy.

How do couples divvy up the housework? Most studies use either a questionnaire or a diary to work out who is doing what. But a 2007 study from Britain compared couples who used both forms and found significant discrepancies between them. The conclusion? "The overall results suggest that there are systematic errors in stylized housework time estimates." Another study compared the self-reporting by husbands and wives and concluded, "Although wives' self-reports differ statistically from the most inclusive ESM [Experience Sampling Method] estimate, husbands' estimates of wives' housework time do not. The mechanisms that produce this similarity are unclear, but it is possible that respondents think about household tasks more globally than do researchers constructing survey questions, and so include in their time estimates *other* activities that they consider as necessary preludes to or components of the household tasks about which they are asked."

You may have had this argument yourself: Should housework be measured by time on task or by effectiveness? What is necessary work, and what is puttering? Should work that is physically taxing, like yard work, count more than work that isn't, like the dishes? Questionnaires and housework diaries deal only in repetitive tasks: sweeping, washing up, mowing the lawn, and so on. What about planning summer vacations? What about figuring out which washer to buy? And what about that far more important but far more vague business of caring? We all know families that are held together because one parent knows who likes what in their sandwiches, who can or cannot read on a road trip, who needs cuddles after a hard day at school. The million tendernesses of "emotion work" all require effort, often thankless effort. They're not going to show up in a housework survey.

Cleanliness, like sex, feels organic while being highly constructed. In Katherine Ashenburg's *The Dirt on Clean*, a study of historical standards of cleanliness, the relativism of hygiene over time is amazing: "Even more than in the eye or the nose, cleanliness exists in the mind of the beholder. Every culture defines it for itself, choosing what it sees as the perfect point between squalid and over-fastidious. . . . It follows that hygiene has always been a convenient stick with which to beat other peoples." The ancient Romans would have found Renaissance Europeans disgusting, as their Muslim contemporaries did. Our early modern forebears saw bathing as an experience rather than a daily practice. But our hygiene would have seemed degraded to the ancestors of even fifty years ago. This transference of physical abjection onto whole categories of human beings remains alive in the various microcultures of big cities, each with its pocket prejudices: who is filthy, who is anal, who smells funny.

There exists no standard definition of *what has to be done* in a household. There is only *what feels so intensely like it needs to be done that it needs to be done.** Difficulties of definition necessarily haunt many sociological studies, but in the case of housework those difficulties press in from all sides.

---

* A brief list of domestic stuff that's on my mind right now, swirling around:

- The fridge leaks sometimes; replace or repair?
- Our daughter is getting big for her toddler bed; I should go online and fine a proper twin bed that will fit in her little room.
- The swim lesson sign-up date is soon.
- Baseball team tryouts are on Tuesday; our son has to remember to pack his glove.
- What healthy snacks will our son actually eat?
- I need to pick up a gift certificate to the comic book store for my son's friend's birthday present.

These all *have to be done*.

In one Canadian study, "What Is Household Work?," the sociologists had the intriguing idea of asking women what they considered their chores to be. A surprising array of answers emerged. For one Iranian Canadian woman it involved calling her sister every day. Overwhelmingly, women maintain the kinship bonds, which require, beyond the shadow of a doubt, immense efforts. Other subjects in the Canadian study mentioned spiritual practices as chores: "Spiritual activities included prayer, meditation, going to church, and participating in healing circles for Aboriginal women. Spirituality was treated as a reason for and a way to care for themselves and the people around them." And why not? Why shouldn't spirituality be considered a domestic duty? If prayers need to be sent, somebody needs to send them.

None of these methodological difficulties or more or less expansive versions of domestic labor excuses male passivity. If anything, they show how much more women are doing and how much of it is forgotten—simply not registered in the accounts of what goes into the day. But how do you tally up caring and prayer? The "moral dimension" to housework, as some feminist scholars have called it, complicates all merely economic readings of the situation. Nancy Folbre, an economist at the University of Massachusetts, has been arguing for years that the measure of gross domestic product should include some reflection of the vast economy of unpaid labor that takes place in the home. The method she suggests for establishing the value of that labor is to take the time devoted to unpaid housework and multiply it by the worker's market wage. The question then becomes "How much would it have cost if you had hired a nanny or a maid to do it?" Folbre is well aware of the limits of this methodology, but that doesn't hide the fundamental error that makes the question mostly nonsense. Housework is not alienated labor. In its emotional dimension, it is not work you can hire somebody to do. Technological progress has saved immense labor in the home over the past one hundred years; it hasn't stopped arguments, though. If money and technology could solve the problem, they already would have, at least for those who can afford to pay. Couples merely shift the battleground: people with dishwashers go from fighting about who cleans the dishes to fighting about who empties the dishwasher; people with nannies fight about who manages the nannies.* And so on.

Difficulties of accounting don't preclude the need for some kind of account, though. By Folbre's analysis, even the domestic tasks for which you can hire labor amount to an unexpressed 25.7 percent of GDP, the bulk of which completely hidden production inordinately falls on women.

---

*I disagree. The brief two-year period when our daughter was an infant and we had a full-time caregiver in our house was pretty terrific. The home was always tidy. We never fought about who was going to unload the dishwasher because our nanny did that. In fact our marriage works best when there are three of us: Steve with his job, me with mine, and a third person who is responsible for running the household, making the beds, doing the laundry, prepping dinner, and taking the kids places. Now that she's gone, I feel like we're scrambling. Always scrambling. I know enough rich people to know that money doesn't solve every problem. But it does solve the problem of who is going to empty the dishwasher.

* * *

My wife has always done more housework than I have. I sense vaguely, half-consciously, all that my wife has done in the times in and around her big job and the kids: the straightened coffee table and the fluffed pillows, the swept floors and organized shelves in the kitchen with their glass jars for salt and sugar and flour, the magazines evenly spaced in the bathroom magazine racks, the coziness that follows a thousand tender putterings. Whole aspects of cleanliness essential to her—a thick line of dust across the bookshelves, the position of the appliances on the kitchen counter—they pass me by completely. I shouldn't say "completely." I notice a messy room, but I don't care. I certainly don't care enough to straighten it myself. I cannot bring myself to care. Or at least not enough, not nearly enough to stop writing this and go down and straighten the room.

When people are young, they think "we'll make a contract.*

---

*I have silently, privately made a vow to myself that I will never fight with Steve about housework. I will never accuse him of forgetting to take out the garbage, or blame him for leaving his dirty lunch dishes in the sink, or ask him how it's possible he never, ever manages to put his dirty socks directly into the laundry basket but tosses them on the floor near the laundry basket so that I have to pick them up. Why? (1) Such fights are so boring, so predictable, so familiar, and so utterly pointless I can't bear to have them or hear myself initiate them. They go like this: My accusation ("How could you have left three dirty cups in the living room?"), his defensive response that usually involves an angry itemization of all the things he has done to benefit the family in the past day or so, my passive-aggressive silent treatment at the fact

Household contracts are well-suited to the technocratic young people who have it together enough to move in with one another. The thinking goes like this: We have a problem—a fair division of housework—therefore we need a solution: a contract. We want to avoid subservience, therefore we will provide means to mutual obedience to a mutual will. The enlightened legalism has a satisfying finality to it. Every couple who draws up a domestic contract thinks they have finally figured out adulthood. They cheerfully imitate their elders and draw up to-do lists and concomitant schedules, which they then post in a neutral place. Sometimes they even go so far as to sign these documents.

―――――――――――――――――――――――――――――――

that he won't just admit that maybe he should have picked up after himself, the lack of resolution, the sour air that lingers, the failure to improve the conditions of our marriage. (2) The fact that Steve is kind of right: he does do a million things each day for the sake of the family and does have a lot of credit in the bank and maybe it's okay if he leaves his dirty coffee cups around the living room when he's the one who picked our son up from school because I'm at work and he's the one that is going to take the kids to the park after dinner to give me the only forty-five minutes of quiet I'll get all day before the bath-story-bed routine and he's the one that is going to stay up late working to earn money that we can put into the children's education fund that he set up and keeps an eye on. Maybe it's okay that I do a little more around the house because overall it kind of evens out. So now when I find that he has managed to leave three of his sweaters lying around the living room, I just pick them up, take them upstairs, fold them, and put them in a pile, and instead of getting mad, I think about the fact that Steve spends half an hour or more each evening helping our nine-year-old with his homework. I never help with homework. I'm better at picking up sweaters.

Sarah and I did not go that far, but we had contracts worked out in fine detail: who did what when, with weekly tasks in rotation. It was strictly the hard stuff: cleaning toilets, scrubbing bathtubs, sweeping floors, doing dishes. Equality remained as elusive as ever. The contract is only as solid as the terms of its interpretation. The question of what constitutes a clean bathtub has as many answers as there are people. What happens when one person rushes and the other lingers? Because you can tell the difference. But there are deeper problems as well; housework by contract is like sex on a schedule: it misses the point of the action. If a relationship is about contracts and schedules, it is rational. But if you have only a rational relationship, why are you bothering? You'll do better with hookers and cleaning ladies—the costs and benefits are more clearly aligned. We want intimacy in love, a house full of intimate love, and intimacy cannot be a contractual economy. It wants gifts. Even in households with domestic contracts, what both sides desire is a gift over and above the contract, the necessary but not required, obvious but not expected gesture.

* * *

Housework is intimate drudgery. Understanding its intimacy is at least as important as understanding its drudgery.

As women make more money, they do more housework. There are several conflicting explanations for why this result consistently appears in studies on the subject, but the most widely accepted is that women who perform breadwinner functions try to compensate for that public role in private. The study that identified this "gender deviance neutralization" was undertaken in Australia: "While Australian women reduce their housework time as their share of couple income approaches equality, past the point of equal income shares, these women actually increase their housework time. This U-shaped relationship between income share and housework time seems to support the idea that women who are gender deviant in income may seek to neutralize that deviance through the performance of gender through housework." Thus the peculiar middle-class ritual of cleaning up for the cleaning lady. Even if women pay for the performance of traditionally female functions, they still need to prove their ability to perform those functions. (Even writing down the list of the chores I have done, I feel slightly emasculated. My gonads shrink into my body a bit.)

Research into "gender neutralization" in housework has shown outliers in certain countries, such as Sweden and Great Britain, although the evidence for a U-shaped curve between income share and housework does apply in the United States. Another study broadened the theory to include not just income as an instance of "gender deviance" but the gender type of the work involved, which showed an even stronger correlation: "Men and women perform gender through the routine activities of male- and female-typed housework and this performance appears to be undertaken in part to neutralize the gender deviance created when men and women are employed in gender-atypical occupations." What constitutes gender deviance in the professions at the moment will no doubt alter with time. Fifty years ago a "woman doctor" was an unusual phenomenon. Now not so much. Nonetheless, compensatory performances, intimate, tucked away, continue to affect daily domestic life. A woman who works at a traditionally male job tries to be more traditionally female at home. A man who is at home compensates by being less of a homemaker.

Like everything in marriage, the division of domestic duties ultimately boils down to sex, the fundamental struggle to achieve regulated passion. In what must be one of the most widely reported sociological studies in history, a team of researchers in 2012 reported that men who do housework have less sex than men who don't, and men who do traditional male "work around the house," like yard work, have more sex than men who don't. That old chestnut of sex advice columns, that tidying up the kitchen will get your wife in the mood, is sadly inaccurate. Women may think they want a man who sweeps floors, and they may really want one around, but, in general, they don't want one in bed. It's a discomfiting, somewhat humiliating, somewhat thrilling way of looking at housework. Chores are the world's dreariest form of foreplay.

Housework is a stumbling block in the comedy of society at large as much as in the comedy of personal life. The subject has always been a hiccup in the grand rhetoric of women's liberation. Even John Stuart Mill in his work on the subjugation of women stumbled over its unique societal position. Mill was a classic good liberal: he believed that marriage should be based on rational love between equals; he believed in the education of women. But he also quite casually assumed that women would always remain at home, in their natural domain, out of choice.

This has led more than a few people to question the point of women's liberation if the end result is to raise better servants.

Even Marx and Engels, the grandest of all theorists of labor relations, struggled to agree on a definition. Housework, said Marx, did not fall under the category of alienated labor, like most other forms of production in capitalist life, but belonged to the realm of craft, the humanizing and personalizing of space. So under communism people do housework. Engels believed the opposite, that housework would eventually be industrialized, and hence simply erased from the coming utopia.

Feminism has more or less inherited this double view, unsure whether to celebrate housework as unappreciated "women's work" or to condemn it as a kind of societal imprisonment. The clean or the dirty house lies between the street and the bedroom. On the street there should be justice, but desire is never fair. Here an almost existential despair sets in. There is no solution to the economic injustice of housework, any more than there is a solution to human desire.

* * *

I do not remember any arguments in my childhood home about the nature of gender essentialism or the patriarchal structures latent in a capitalist society, no disquisitions about female objectification or the inherent violence of patriarchy or the advent of third-wave after second-wave feminism. I do remember my mother and father fighting about who cleaned up, or rather they would fight about something that had nothing to do with cleaning up but was really about who was vacuuming the floors. Such arguments were an inevitable part of progress, the tensions of the past they were attempting to shrug off.

Housework was what my mother was raised to do; escaping it meant escaping a gendered fate. I am her son, and yet her story barely seems from my own time or my own country. Her parents in rural New Brunswick didn't teach her to drive; that was for men. Her parents didn't want her to be a doctor, either; that too was for men. She attended university on a home economics scholarship and then surreptitiously transferred into botany. In that, even then, at the beginning of her journey, was a bargain she struck with the old orders: she mastered the material conditions of home economics so that, under cover, she could see the larger beauties of life. My mother stuck to that deal for the whole of her life. While building a fully functioning practice as a physician, she more or less ran a household as if she were a housewife. She cooked dinner every night. She maintained, as in my grandparents' house, a parlor, a room set aside not to be touched, simply to be clean. In the parlor, behind a glass partition, the prettiest things in the house were never touched: the Psyanka eggs her Ukrainian patients brought her in gratitude, ivory carvings from our family trip to China, the porcelain she inherited from her grandmother. Domestic totems, as direct and noisy as animist shrines. Behold, I have money! Behold, I am clean! Behold, I am a woman! Behold, I have fulfilled the sacred duties!

The house-beast in which I grew up was hungrier than the house-beast in which I currently live. It was a house built on the principle of the Canadian prairie: There's space enough here to fit us all in. The wide sprawl of its hallways made a kind of suburb inside the house inside the suburbs. Our living room, off to a half-sunken side, was as large as the entire ground floor of my current house. And my mother vacuumed it all, weekly, in between delivering babies and encountering sickness and death, being on call. Supermomdom was less an overturning of gender roles than their doubling: do everything that a man was expected to do in 1955 while also doing everything that a woman was expected to do in 1955. The obligations remained, more or less, fully intact.

And now I remember Halloween costumes, hand-made Halloween costumes.* My chubby eight-year-old self in a Hobbit costume that made me look like a Franciscan monk. My brother as an owl. As ludicrous as it sounds, working

---

* Most of my friends buy their kids factory-made Halloween costumes or used ones picked up at garage sales. My colleague, a well-paid professional woman, has a five-year-old daughter who this year wanted to be a Marvel comic book hero so obscure that the costume was not available at Walmart. A craft was required. My colleague is good at crafts but had no time to give the project the attention it needed, so she hired an art school student to make the costume with her daughter over a couple of weekends in October. This is a growing trend. You can hire people to teach your kid to ride a bicycle. In my neighborhood there's a young woman who is regularly hired to coach kids on their third grade homework assignments—building bridges with popsicle sticks and that type of thing. Is it wrong to outsource these mother-type and father-type jobs if you can afford to? Not to me.

mothers in the 1980s in North America were fully expected to make their children's Halloween costumes. To buy one was a sign of failure. One Halloween my mother-in-law, a radio producer responsible for four kids, hand-stitched an entire bumblebee costume out of strips of cloth. Sarah walked to the first house on the left, the neighbor said, "Aren't you a nice convict," and Sarah walked home, cried in her room, and refused to go out again that night. From the middle of my own harried parenthood, all this crafty business—the expectation that professional women will sew—seems like mild madness.

My mother's housework responsibilities were no doubt compounded by living in a house full of rambunctious boys. My father was a tolerated bumbler in the domestic sphere. His efforts were vital, however. Our efforts too were vital, the boys' efforts. An odd kind of chivalry was involved: cleaning up was a noble gesture to try to keep Mom from being overwhelmed. Was that progress? Pseudo-progress? I have no idea. Or is all progress pseudo-progress?

The psychology of housework is nostalgic, inevitably—attempting to re-create or avoid the ecology of our childhood. Pulling away from the way we are used to doing things is a slow extraction out of a sticky business. Atavism is as inevitable as progress because the household cleanliness we are used to does not feel like an inheritance any more than our genes do. The household's cleanliness or dirtiness feels like an organic state of being. We all just want to feel at home.

* * *

Despite many failures, mostly mine, there is a much more equal breakdown in our household tasks than in our parents' houses. What constitutes the progress? Is it that I do slightly more housework than my father, or that our house is less demanding? Or is it that we have lower standards?

Right at the beginning of the modern feminist movement, in *The Second Sex*, Simone de Beauvoir identified housework as the key impediment to the liberation of women: "Woman is doomed to the continuation of the species and the care of the home." Women's sexual status as objects, their ineligibility to own property, their exclusion from the world of work, even immobilizing fashions—for de Beauvoir, they are all rooted in the original constitution of woman as the maintainer of the home. Her descriptions of housework are blistering in their hatred: "Few tasks are more like the torture of Sisyphus than housework, with its endless repetition: the clean becomes soiled, the soiled is made clean, over and over, day after day. The housewife wears herself out marking time: she makes nothing, simply perpetuates the present. . . . Washing, ironing, sweeping, ferreting out fluff from under the wardrobes—all this halting of decay is also the denial of life; for time simultaneously creates and destroys, and only its negative aspect concerns the housekeeper." It is worth noting that for de Beauvoir, who has several ideas for improving marriage with utopian sexual arrangements, there is no suggestion that housework should be divided equally. Housework is oppression in itself. "The healthy young woman will hardly be attracted by so gloomy a vice," she writes. Radical feminists like Angela Davis find hope in the possibility of changing social standards. In "The Approaching Obsolescence of Housework: A Working-Class Perspective," she writes, "Although housework as we know it today may eventually become a bygone relic of history, prevailing social attitudes continue to associate the eternal female condition with images of brooms and dustpans, mops and pails, aprons and stoves, pots and pans. And it is true that women's work, from one historical era to another, has been associated in general with the homestead. Yet female domestic labour has not always been what it is today, for like all social phenomena, housework is a fluid product of human history."

In our own time healthy young women seem attracted more than ever to the "gloomy vice" of housework. In the ideal life the female lawyer comes home to the midcentury-modern living room, with the books organized by color. Maybe when she makes partner she'll buy that Le Corbusier lamp she's always wanted, the one that inspired Kanye West. Or at least a decent reproduction. Needless to say, the female lawyer does less housework than her stay-at-home mom did, but that does not prevent the desire for vacuumed blinds, for an organized crisper, for the shelf in the kitchen island—the kind Martha Stewart has—filled with copper cookie cutters in various shapes. And this despite the fact that, from the very first studies of the sociology of housework, women who work out of their home are more satisfied in their lives than women who work in it.

The bizarre reality of women making their own candles, knitting, and raising chickens coincides neatly with the rise of working women who actually do much less housework. Martha Stewart has made an empire out of immanence. The fetishization of the domestic is everywhere. Hillary Clinton's major source of relaxation, according to the *New York Times*, is *Love It or List It*, a reality show on Home and Garden Television in which a renovator fixes up a couple's old place while a real estate agent finds them a new place, and the couple has to choose between the two.

Housework entertainment naturally is compensation. The fantasy of the domesticity channels is of an old-fashioned domestic intimacy. The food on FoodTV isn't hypermodern fusion; it's classic comfort food. When a female celebrity reaches a certain level of popularity, she founds a home-based lifestyle website: Gwyneth Paltrow, Reese Witherspoon, Jessica Alba, Blake Lively, and on and on. The domesticity fantasy is about having the luxury to care about the details of our own or other people's lives. It is about the joy of family life without the unmanageableness. It is inherently nostalgic, antiprogress. Housework is the macho bullshit of women. And, in this light, it is perhaps not surprising that men have not started doing more housework. Men might be willing to lose the garbage of their own gender stereotypes, but why should they take on the garbage of another?

Equality is coming, but not the way we expected. The future does not involve men doing more housework. A recent study of transgendered men found that housework is divided inequitably even in that group. There is a slight correlation between the egalitarianism of a household and a fairer division of domestic labor, but the most substantial correlation is that the more egalitarian a household is, the less housework gets done altogether. Men's behavior may not be changing, but here is the good news: women's is. The sociologist Suzanne M. Bianchi and her colleagues identified this trend as early as 2000: "Time-diary data from representative samples of American adults show that the number of overall hours of domestic labor (excluding child care and shopping) has continued to decline steadily and predictably since 1965. This finding is mainly due to dramatic declines among women (both in and out of the paid labor market), who have cut their housework hours almost in half since the 1960s."

By Folbre's calculation, the proportion of unpaid domestic labor in relation to the overall economy has declined from 39 percent in 1965 to 25.7 percent in 2010. Because women are doing less and less, the difference between the amount of housework that men and women do continues to narrow. And not because women are so busy they can't do the housework. Bianchi et al. reported that "the likelihood of doing housework was, if anything, declining fastest for those with the most time available for domestic work."

The psychological term for this process is *disinvestment*. Not that disinvestment helps anyone who lives in a house with others, anymore than tectonic shifts help the flower now growing in the alpine meadow. The trends in history leave us behind in our place, to struggle toward our own balance of expectation and gift on the terms of our own inheritance. Domestic arrangements exist to protect us from the trends anyway. Shelter is from change as much as from the elements.

* * *

Caring less is the hope of the future. Housework is perhaps the only political problem in which doing less and not caring are the solution, where apathy is the most progressive and sensible attitude. Fifty years ago it was perfectly normal to iron sheets and vacuum drapes; they were necessary tasks. The solution to the inequalities of dusting wasn't dividing the dusting; it was not doing the dusting at all. The solution to the gender divide in housework generally is that simple: Don't bother. Leave the stairs untidy. Don't fix the garden gate. Fail to repaint the stained ceiling. Never make the bed.

Housework is both the symbol and the substance of the fate of men and women in their intimate lives. The political struggle is more or less beside the point. Educating men to be domestic has failed, and yet subterranean and economic forces are making equality more real every day. And as these waves of change crash against us, we see what crumbles and what sticks, what we really need and what is mostly an act, what we care about and what we pretend to care about, what belongs to us and what is only visiting, who we are and who we just thought we were.

A clean house is the sign of a wasted life, truly. Eventually we'll all be living in perfect egalitarian squalor.

EIGHT

—

Messy Hope

SOMETIMES I wake up late and lie in bed listening to the voices of my wife and son and daughter on the ground floor.* The sound of the negotiation of breakfast and home-

---

*It's 7:51 a.m. and I've locked myself in the bathroom to write this note. I haven't showered yet. My son is finishing up his homework; my daughter is creating a fortress with her Magformers. All our beds are unmade. I need to shower and get into an outfit that will make me look like a capable grown-up. I need to grab Steve for two minutes before I leave to discuss who is picking up whom after school and what they're going to have for dinner before my mom arrives to babysit the kids. The to-do list is epic. And yet I wouldn't want it any other way. Before I had kids I read several books about Why Happiness Eludes the Modern Woman. They said that feminism and motherhood were incompatible. They said that working and taking care of kids was too exhausting to be handled. They were wrong. You can make it work, and even love your life, if (1) you find a partner who, as Ruth Bader Ginsburg famously says, values your career as much as his own, and (2) you give up on the 1980s myth of being the always-perfect-at-everything supermom. I lucked out on 1 and I'm working on 2.

work and schedule muffled and funneled by the particular tim-
bre of the house is a beautiful, ordinary sound, but I know that
a vast historical struggle underlies its ordinariness, a centuries-
long political struggle for the chance to have the problems of
human beings: sex and ambition, school worries, squabbling,
cooking meals, sweeping floors, the messiness of the mingled
miracle and catastrophe of men and women together. The tur-
moil is so much more than political. The rearrangement of
ideas, and even of economic reality, runs above the rearrangement of bodies: the new ones come; the new ones become the
old ones; the old ones go.

The split between power and intimacy defined gender for
millennia: men in the realm of power, women in the realm
of intimacy. My parents lived the great tumult of the 1960s
and 1970s that brought power and intimacy together, but they
lived it from the margins; my mother spent the Summer of
Love at medical school, while my father was at Royal Military
College, about as square as it comes. When they settled down,
they settled in a classic suburban house in a prosperous midsize
city, the kind with a two-car garage and a lawn that took me the
better part of an afternoon to mow and that could have been
decorated with a massive banner inscribed "We Are Normal."

Their quiet life was possible only after many revolutions.
They were exactly the kind of apolitical people Carol Hanisch
was describing in "The Personal Is Political." They were far from
the movements of their time, yet the facts of their lives—most
notably my mother's job as a doctor—amounted to novelty in
the sphere of gender relations. It was not ideas that set them

forward but the pursuit of personal fulfillment, and the pursuit of personal fulfillment has more radical consequences than ideas ever could.

The divide between the worlds of power and intimacy, or between the worlds of work and family, broke down of its own accord. My father did paperwork while he watched my soccer games because he had no choice. My mother had her kids wandering the hospital or sleeping in the parking lot while she delivered babies because that was how it worked out. My father learned to cook (or sort of cook—I remember spaghetti and tomato sauce with peanuts added for protein) because my mother was on call. My mother had to be on call to pay the mortgage. Worlds collided out of the ambition of their lives and their need to ride the opportunities of the economic expansion of the postwar period.

The bleeding of the private into the public and of the intimate with work and power was the most radical force of the second half of the twentieth century. It altered and keeps altering human nature. But perhaps what is most surprising about the intertwining of the intimate and the political over the past fifty years is how natural it has felt. We have learned that patriarchy is as artificial as any other mode of life. The assumptions that have crumbled have left new insights in their place, insights that nobody could have predicted. It would not have seemed possible that working mothers would be as attentive and responsive and satisfied in their family lives as stay-at-home mothers, but they are. It would not have seemed possible that fathers would fight to spend more time with their kids, but they do.

Our ancestors left a few buried hints of these possibilities. In "The Wife of Bath's Tale" Chaucer tells the story of a knight on a quest to discover what women want. He crosses the earth and hears hundreds of answers from hundreds of women, but when he is asked for a one-word conclusion, he doesn't hesitate: "Sovereignty." Women want power. And as for the tenderness of new fatherhood, one of the most touching scenes in the whole of *The Iliad* is when the great hero Hektor has a last visit with his son Astyanax before heading to certain death in battle against Achilles.

> Hektor held out his arms
> To take his baby. But the child squirmed round
> On the nurse's bosom and began to wail,
> Terrified by his father's great war helm—
> The flashing bronze, the crest with horsehair plume
> Tossed like a living thing at every nod.
> His father began laughing, and his mother
> Laughed as well. Then from his handsome head
> Hektor lifted off his helm and bent
> To place it, bright with sunlight, on the ground.
> When he had kissed his child and swung him high
> To dandle him, he said [a] prayer.

In the ancient martial epic, a story of mass slaughter, the warrior takes off his helmet to cuddle his infant son.

* * *

Predictions are messages that writers send to the future so the world will know how blind and arrogant they are now. But any serious consideration of the trends as they appear at the moment has to be more than optimistic; it should be delirious with hope. Equality is coming, bumpily but surely. Women's economic and political clout is constantly increasing; violence against women is constantly declining; family roles are constantly broadening; the housework gap is constantly narrowing. These trends are deep and of a piece and decades old. They are transforming business and politics and daily life.

The forces altering the lives of men and women have little to do with ideas. The rise of women in the workplace, the emerging diversity of family values—they didn't happen because people suddenly came to their senses under the impetus of a grand enlightenment. Hope is born in the marketplace and under covers and behind closed doors; it isn't spearheaded by movements or Twitter. Economic and technological change has blazed a crooked path, and we are playing intellectual catch-up, poorly. The often invisible processes blithely transform who we are, unimpeded by debate, and an invisible triumph rolls underneath a pointless, aestheticized rage. The time has come to recognize that the current we are riding is taking us to a fuller humanity for men and women, to a deeper intimacy and more equal sharing of power. We are getting what we want. We are becoming who we are supposed to be.

Simone de Beauvoir begins *The Second Sex* with a clear vision of the whole of humanity, not just of women: "Every individual concerned with justifying his existence experiences his existence as an indefinite need to transcend himself." The situation of women, de Beauvoir saw, was the denial and restriction of the capacity for transcendence and self-determination that men took for granted. "She discovers and chooses herself in a world where men force her to assume herself as Other. An attempt is made to freeze her as an object and doom her to immanence."

Doomed to immanence—such a precise phrase. Doomed to belong to others. Doomed to be of the earth and of blood and bone. Doomed to be rooted. The half-distinct shuffling of the house beneath me—that is the immanence to which I am doomed. My daughter and my son and my wife in the house, the minor ecology of family life, hands crossed behind the back just like the dead great-grandfather in a photograph, elbows skinned to the same roughness thirty years apart, the shared flutter of eyelashes, the mutual moods that flash up like birdcalls, wild urgings that race past the horizon, the underground caverns hollowed out by long-forgotten histories, disappointments half tucked away, and the geological pressures of money, the glare of outsiders looking in, and all the inexplicable and inconceivable wave and ebb we give the name of family. That is bodily love, the doom of immanence. The faint odor of toddler shit—utterly abject and succulent at once—means you must go upstairs and change her. The angry curl of hunger means you must feed him. The wail in the night means you must rise to comfort the wailer. The easing of the day and the leavening exhaustion means that you must sleep.

De Beauvoir imagined the achievement of equality as women escaping immanence. But we have learned since the rise of women that we're all doomed to immanence, men and women both. And not only that, but we need our immanence. We crave it. Each of us, one by one, will have to ride the turbulence between the body and dreams, between desire and justice, between the world as it has always been and the world as it might turn out to be.

* * *

"A woman needs a man like a fish needs a bicycle." This is true. But the fish and the bicycle still fall in love. The fish and the bicycle still sleep together. The fish and the bicycle make coffee for each other in the morning and chat and pick out furniture together. The fish and the bicycle have children.

The fish and the bicycle still get married. The ideal of marriage has survived the rearrangement of intimate life. Only 12 percent of unmarried Americans say they want to stay that way, and 93 percent of married Americans believe that love is the most important reason to get married. At the same time, marriage is becoming more select, a decision made after careful consideration of all the options. Increasingly it is a privilege for those with money and education and experience. The marrieds keep getting older and older: in 2013 only 24 percent of Americans between eighteen and thirty-two were married; the rate was 36 percent in 1997, 48 percent in 1980, and 65 percent in 1960. Since 1970 marriage rates have declined steadily among the less affluent, but not among top income earners. "Assortative mating," as the sociologists call it, is one of the major engines of America's exploding income inequality: rich people increasingly marry other rich people, whom they meet at college, where rich people get sexually sorted. Being marriageable is no longer a sign that you're ordinary; it's a sign of elite membership, of being a winner. They should change the wedding vows from "To have and to hold, for richer and poorer, in sickness and in health, till death do us part" to "For richer and hopefully much richer, in healthy mutual exchange, to kick the shit out of the world together till it is mutually inconvenient."

These more considered marriages are not colder marriages; they are more connected. Of all the numbers swirling through this book, the most hopeful and the most vital is this: more than 80 percent of Americans feel their family is as close as or closer than the family they grew up in, and only 5 percent feel that their family is less close.

Here is the hope under that hope: equality more accurately reflects the nature of our being, so we may more accurately reflect each other. A relationship is a series of negotiated contracts, of happy or unhappy exchanges, but ultimately two mutually incompatible desires are at play when a self-possessed person wants to lose himself or herself in another. "The first moment in love is that I do not wish to be a self-subsistent and independent person, or that, if I were, then I would feel defective and incomplete," Hegel wrote in *Outlines of the Philosophy of Right* two hundred years ago. "The second moment is that I find myself in another person, that I count for something in another, while the other in turn comes to count for something in me. Love, therefore, is the most tremendous contradiction; the Understanding cannot resolve it."

A good marriage is a transcendent miracle, according to

Hegel. "Marriage so far as its essential basis is concerned, is not a contractual relationship. On the contrary, though marriage begins in contract, it is precisely a contract to transcend the standpoint of contract, the standpoint from which persons are regarded in their individuality." The rearrangement of the twenty-first century, the future of men and women, will rewrite all contracts between the genders, but it will not change our hunger to pass beyond them. We need better contracts mainly in order to forget they were there in the first place.

*   *   *

During wedding ceremonies in the nineteenth century bride and groom remained separate, distinct, and the bride's veil was removed only after the completion of the legal and religious business. After the conclusion of contracts intimacy began. The signed documents, the oral agreements in front of witnesses, were prolegomena to the revelation of the face, a man and woman looking at each other, into each other. Then the mystery.

I know very little about marriage, less and less every year. My mother once told me that the point of marriage is to grow ugly together. I used to think that's why so many romantic comedies end with a wedding, to keep everyone young and beautiful. I'm starting to understand that the reason writers stick to the territory before marriage is that it's easier to figure out.

What nobody tells you about marriage and children is that they make life weirder and weirder. They are not a state of normal complacency, of happily ever after. Take breasts. When you're a kid, breasts can just be breasts. Nobody told Sarah or me that the oxytocin released in sex is the same hormone that causes a letdown of milk during breastfeeding. The first time in bed after the birth of our son, I lay there, coated in small rivers of the world's loveliest but least erotic fluid, while Sarah ran off, giggling, to collect the precious dew of her body in a bottle.* Every drop spilling on me was nourishment not going to the boy. Later he went through a period when he stopped shitting. It was three days, then it was five, then it was ten, then we went to a doctor, who explained that when a baby is exclusively breast-fed, the hormonal cycle between the breast and the child sometimes becomes so complete, so absolutely in sync, that the baby stops needing to excrete for stretches of time. Miraculously the feedback from the saliva in the child's mouth communicates so precisely the needs of his body to the breast it sucks that there is no waste.

The meaning of breasts will change after the intimate revolution. I understand that there are some men, and some women too, who believe that such familiarity drains away the erotic. I could not disagree more. It is better to love breasts than to love décolletage. It is better to love a woman than to love a woman who disguises herself as a woman. The revolutionary moment of men crossing into the delivery room, of men crossing into the biological world of the species, pulling down the many veils the world has put up, has an erotic meaning that extends to the horizon. We get to find out what bodies are really like.

―――――――――――――――――――――――

*Oh my God, that was so messy and so weird and so surprising and so fun.

The revolution of intimacy is possible only because men and women crave intimacy. At the bottom of all the rage and sorrow lies the urge for recognition and for tenderness. Tenderness resists theory. Tenderness embarrasses, mocking accomplishment. Tenderness relishes the embarrassments of the business of living: the piss on the floor, the tears on cheeks that only you can kiss away, hot blood, drool on the pillow, the nest of the shoulder and armpit, the curve of the hip raked by the splurge of infants.

For Sarah and me the rearrangements of our lives—birth and death and jobs and changing cities—matter only because we love each other. I have known Sarah since I was nineteen and she was twenty; we have fallen down around and into each other. Memories grow from their own mush: the constellation of the unpredictable family, the hands of the high school boys, a photograph of her looking out at the sea, a photograph with garbage in Jerusalem, the fact that cats hate her, the occasional longing for pickled herring, the adored teacher who slept with the boys in his class and fascinated her forever. And then there is me, with my unkempt hair and my distraction and the way I cannot help but stare or interrupt, the boy with his hand out. These million subtleties, a million million conservations—long distance, in bed, over sushi, over and in between the chattering children—have not managed to exhaust.

The lives of men and women are filling with a radical hope that remains half-hidden: we might actually find out what being a man and being a woman means. The attempt of men and women to live with each other is an indefinite, never-ending struggle, infinitely complicated. Intimacy complicates. The contracts fall apart: less than entitlement and more than deserving. The primitive golden idol glows in the cave no matter how civilized we become—stupid, stupid love in its idiotic omnipotence.

Meanwhile the primordial crisis is rising for the first time, the crisis that has been lurking for us all, men and women both, from the beginning of the species. What does it mean to be a mammal who wants to change the world?

WHERE THE NUMBERS COME FROM

How Much Should a Man Speak?

PAGE

3   *Mansplaining*: Rebecca Solnit, *Men Explain Things to Me* (New York: Haymarket, 2014).

5   *On women talking more than men*: Louann Brizendine, *The Female Brain* (New York: Broadway Books, 2006); Matthias Mehl, Simine Vazire, Nairan Ramirez-Esparza, Richard B. Slatcher, and James W. Pennebaker, "Are Women Really More Talkative Than Men?," *Science* 317 (2007): 82; Jukka-Pekka Onnela, Benjamin N. Waber, Alex Pentland, Sebastian Schnorf, and David Lazer, "Using Sociometers to Quantify Social Interaction Patterns," *Scientific Reports* 4 (2014): 5604.

6   *Study of email exchanges*: Victor Brajer and Andrew Gill, "Yakity-Yak: What Talks Back? An Email Experiment," *Social Science Quarterly* 91.4 (2010).

6   *Women's domination of social media*: Maeve Duggan, "It's a Woman's (Social Media) World," Pew Research Center, December 9, 2013, www.pewresearch.org/fact-tank/2013/09/12/its-a-womans-social-media-world/.

6   *On male silence*: Jack O. Balswick and Charles W. Peek, "The Inexpressive Male: A Tragedy of American Society," *Family Coordinator* 20.4 (1971): 363–68; Michael McGill, *The McGill Report of Male Intimacy* (New York: Holt, Rinehart

and Winston, 1985); Jack Sattel, "The Inexpressive Male: Tragedy or Sexual Politics?" *Sexual Politics*, 23:4, April 1976, pp. 469–77; Scott and Oates anecdote: in Marilyn J. Landis, *Antarctica: Exploring the Extreme* (Chicago: Chicago Review Press, 2001); Baldessare Castiglione, *The Book of the Courtier*, trans. George Bull (London: Penguin, 1976); Philip quote from Plutarch, *Plutarch on Sparta*, trans. Richard J. A. Talbert (London: Penguin Classics, 1988).

10 *Men-women communication*: Deborah Tannen, *You Just Don't Understand* (New York: William Morrow, 2007).

ONE The Hollow Patriarchy

20 *Academic degrees of women and men*: U.S. Census 2012, table 299, www.census.gov/prod/2011pubs/12statab/educ.pdf.

20 *Women dominate in growth industries*: U.S. Department of Labor, Bureau of Labor Statistics, "The 30 Occupations with the Largest Projected Employment Growth, 2010–2020," February 2012, www.bls.gov/news.release/ecopro .t06.htm.

20 *Women as breadwinners*: Wendy Wang, Kim Parker, and Paul Taylor, "Breadwinner Moms," Pew Research Center, May 29, 2013, www.pewsocialtrends.org/2013/05/29/breadwinner -moms/.

20 *The pay gap*: U.S. Department of Labor, Bureau of Labor Statistics, "Women in the Labor Force: A Databook," 2011, www.bls.gov/cps/wlf-databook2011.htm; U.S. Department of Labor, Bureau of Labor Statistics, "Women's Earnings as a Percent of Men's in 2010," January 10, 2012, www.bls.gov /opub/ted/2012/ted_20120110.htm; Pew Research Center, "On Pay Gap, Millennial Women Near Parity—For Now," December 11, 2013, www.pewsocialtrends.org/files/2013/12 /gender-and-work_final.pdf; PwC, "International Women's

Day: PwC Women in Work Index," March 2013. Accessible from here: hdl.voced.edu.au/10707/401343.

21 *The Forbes list*: Andrea Navarro, "The World's Richest Women 2014," *Forbes*, March 3, 2104, www.forbes.com/sites /andreanavarro/2014/03/03/the-worlds-richest-women-2014/.

21 *Percentages of men and women in the professions*: Martha S. West and John W. Curtis, "AAUP Gender Equity Indicators 2006," AAUP, 2006, www.aaup.org/NR/rdonlyres/63396944-44BE -4ABA-9815-5792D93856F1/0/AAUPGenderEquityIndica tors2006.pdf; U.S. Census Bureau, "Census Bureau Re-leases Equal Opportunity Tabulation That Provides a Profile of America's Workforce," November 29, 2012, www.census .gov/newsroom/releases/archives/employment_occupations/cb 12-225.html; U.S. Census Bureau, "2008–2010 American Community Survey 3-Year Estimates," October 27, 2011, www .census.gov/newsroom/releases/archives/american_community _survey_acs/cb11-tps40.html; Julie Triedman, "A Few Good Women," *American Lawyer*, May 28, 2015; Roger Cheng, "Women in Tech: The Numbers Don't Add Up," CNET, May 6, 2015, www.cnet.com/news/women-in-tech-the-numbers -dont-add-up/.

21 *Female board membership*: PwC, "International Women's Day, PwC Women in Work Index."

22 *Women in political office*: World Economic Forum, "Global Gender Gap Report 2014," http://reports.weforum.org /global-gender-gap-report-2014/; National Women's Political Caucus statistics as reported in *Why Congress Needs Women*, ed. Michele A. Paludi (Washington: ABC-CLIO, 2016).

26 *Decisions in the home*: Pew Research Center, "Women Call the Shots at Home: Public Mixed on Gender Roles in Jobs," September 25, 2008,www.pewsocialtrends.org/2008 /09/25/women-call-the-shots-at-home-public-mixed-on-gender -roles-in-jobs/.

27 *Gender in China and OECD*: James Farrer, *Opening Up*

(Chicago: University of Chicago Press, 2002); Leta Hong Fincher, *Leftover Women: The Resurgence of Gender Inequality in China* (New York: Zed Books, 2014); OECD, "Women and Men in OECD Countries," n.d., www.oecd.org/std /37962502.pdf.

28 *International Monetary Fund report*: Katrin Elborgh-Woytek, Monique Newiak, Kalpana Kochhar, Stefania Fabrizio, Kangni Kpodar, Philippe Wingender, Benedict Clements, and Gerd Schwartz, "Women, Work and the Economy: Macroeconomic Gains from Gender Equity," International Monetary Fund, September 2013, www.imf.org/external/pubs/ft/sdn/2013/sdn 1310.pdf.

28 *Goldman Sachs study*: Sandra Lawson, "Women Hold Up Half the Sky," Global Economics Paper No. 164, Goldman Sachs, March 4, 2008, www.goldmansachs.com/our-thinking /investing-in-women/bios-pdfs/women-half-sky-pdf.pdf.

29 *Patriarchy in Japan*: World Economic Forum, "Global Gender Gap Report 2014"; Jonathan Soble, "Abe Pushes for More Women in Senior Roles," *Financial Times*, April 19, 2013.

30 *Genital mutilation*: Heather L. Sipsma, Peggy G. Chen, Angela Ofori-Atta, Ukwuoma O. Ilozumba, Kapouné Karfo, and Elizabeth H. Bradley, "Female Genital Cutting: Current Practices and Beliefs in Western Africa," *Bulletin of the World Health Organization*, November 2011, www.who.int/bulletin /volumes/90/2/11-090886/en/.

30 *Missing women*: Amartya Sen, "More Than 100 Million Women Are Missing," *New York Review of Books*, December 20, 1990.

30 *Boys receive more education than girls*: UNESCO, "World Atlas of Gender Equality in Education," 2012, www.uis.unesco .org/Education/Documents/unesco-world-atlas-gender-educa tion-2012.pdf.

38 *Modern parenthood*: Kim Parker and Wendy Wang, "Modern Parenthood," March 14, 2013, Pew Research Center, www

.pewsocialtrends.org/2013/03/14/modern-parenthood-roles-of
-moms-and-dads-converge-as-they-balance-work-and-family/;
Alex Williams, "Just Wait Until Your Mother Gets Home," *New
York Times*, August 10, 2012, www.nytimes.com/2012/08/12
/fashion/dads-are-taking-over-as-full-time-parents.html?_r=0.

40   *Child care*: U.S. Department of Health and Human Services, "The NICHD Study of Early Child Care and Youth
Development," 2006, www.nichd.nih.gov/publications/pubs
/documents/seccyd_06.pdf; RAND Europe, "Use of Child-
care in the EU Member States and Progress towards the
Barcelona Targets," Short Statistical Report No. 1, April
2014, http://ec.europa.eu/justice/gender-equality/files/docu
ments/140502_gender_equality_workforce_ssr1_en.pdf; Lilian
V. Faulhaber, "How the I.R.S. Hurts Mothers," *New York Times*,
April 3, 2013.

40   *The gender gap among millennials*: Pew Research Center, "On
Pay Gap, Millennial Women Near Parity—For Now."

41   *Maternity leave*: Abt Associates, "Family and Medical Leave in
2012: Detailed Results Appendix," revised April 18, 2014, www
.dol.gov/asp/evaluation/fmla/FMLA-Detailed-Results-Ap
pendix.pdf; "Longer Maternity Leave Is Hurting Women's
Careers, Says Equality Watchdog," *Telegraph*, July 14, 2008, www
.telegraph.co.uk/news/uknews/2403726/Longer-maternity
-leaving-is-hurting-womens-careers-says-equality-watchdog
.html.

43   *Gender diversity on corporate boards*: Gwladys Fouché, "A
Woman's Place Is . . . on the Board," *Guardian*, August 10,
2005, www.theguardian.com/business/2005/aug/10/work
andcareers.genderissues; McKinsey & Company, "Women
Matter: Gender Diversity, a Corporate Performance Driver,"
2007, www.raeng.org.uk/publications/other/women-matter
-oct-2007; Corinne Post and Kris Byron, "Women on Boards
and Financial Performance: Meta-analysis," *Academy of
Management Journal*, August 2015.

47   *2011 study of millennials*: Wendy Wang and Paul Taylor, "For Millennials, Parenthood Trumps Marriage," Pew Research Center, March 9, 2011, www.pewsocialtrends.org/2011/03/09 /for-millennials-parenthood-trumps-marriage/.

48   *Sigmar Gabriel quote*: http://www.theguardian.com/world/2014 /jan/05/german-vice-chancellor-sigmar-gabriel-time-off-dad.

49   *Anne-Marie Slaughter quote:* Anne-Marie Slaughter, *Unfinished Business* (New York: Random House, 2015).

TWO The New Fatherhood

55   *Fathers spending time with their children*: Parker and Wang, "Modern Parenthood."

55   *Desire to have children*: "The Match.com Single in America Study 2011," *Uptodate*, http://blog.match.com/singles -study/. This study was commissioned by a corporation, but it was undertaken by Helen Fisher, a biological anthropologist, and Stephanie Coontz and the University of Binghamton's Institute of Evolutionary Studies. For the study on depression in men and women without children, Robin Hadley of Keele University presented the research at the British Sociological Association annual conference on April 3, 2013. As reported in Sarah Glynn, "Men More Depressed Than Women if Childless," *Medical News Today*, April 4, 2013, www .medicalnewstoday.com/articles/258531.php.

55   *Families without fathers*: U.S. Census Bureau, "Living Arrangements of Children: 1960 to Present," figure CH-1, 2011, www .census.gov/hhes/families/files/graphics/CH-1.pdf; Centre for Social Justice, "Lone Parents Tally Heads for Two Million as Numbers Rise 20,000 a Year, Says CSJ Report," press release, n.p., www.centreforsocialjustice.org.uk/UserStorage/pdf/ Press%20releases%202013/CSJ-Press-Release-Lone-Parents.pdf.

56   *Fatherlessness as social disaster*: U.S. Department of Health and

Human Services, "HHS Launches 'Be Their Dad' Parental Responsibility Campaign," press release, March 26, 1999, http://archive.hhs.gov/news/press/1999pres/990326.html; U.S. Department of Justice, "What Can the Federal Government Do to Decrease Crime and Revitalize Communities?," January 5–7, 1998, www.ncjrs.gov/pdffiles/172210.pdf; N. M. Astone and S. McLanahan, "Family Structure, Parental Practices and High School Completion," *American Sociological Review* 56.3 (1991): 309–20; Nancy Vaden-Kiernan, Nicholas S. Ialongo, Jane Pearson, and Sheppard Kellam, "Household Family Structure and Children's Aggressive Behavior: A Longitudinal Study of Urban Elementary School Children," *Journal of Abnormal Child Psychology* 23.5 (1995): 553–68; David Autor and Melanie Wasserman, "Wayward Sons: The Emerging Gender Gap in Labor Markets and Education," *Third Way*, 2013, http://economics.mit.edu/files/8754; G. R. Weitoft, A. Hjern, B. Haglund, and M. Rosen, "Mortality, Severe Morbidity, and Injury in Children Living with Single Parents in Sweden: A Population-Based Study," *Lancet* 361.9354 (2003): 289–95; James M. Herzog, *Father Hunger: Explorations with Adults and Children* (New York: Routledge, 2014).

56   *Family structure and economic mobility*: Raj Chetty, Nathaniel Hendren, Patrick Kline, and Emmanuel Saez, "Where Is the Land of Opportunity? The Geography of Intergenerational Mobility in the United States," June 2014, www.equality-of -opportunity.org/images/mobility_geo.pdf.

64   *ad anecdotes*: Huggies etc., as reported in Paul Raeburn, *Do Fathers Matter?: What Science is Telling Us About the Parent We've Overlooked* (New York: Macmillan, 2014).

66   *U.S. divorce rates*: Rose M. Kreider and Renee Ellis, "Number, Timing, and Duration of Marriages and Divorces: 2009," *Current Population Reports*, May 2011, www.census.gov /prod/2011pubs/p70-125.pdf.

66   *Changing opinions of gay marriage*: Justin McCarthy, "Same-

Sex Marriage Support Reaches New High at 55%," Gallup, May 21, 2014, www.gallup.com/poll/169640/sex-marriage -support-reaches-new-high.aspx; Peter Wallsten and Scott Wilson, "Obama endorses gay marriage," *Washington Post*, May 9, 2012; Sarah McBride, "Mozilla CEO resigns, opposition to gay marriage drew fire," Reuters, April 3, 2014; Pew Research Center, "Support for Same Sex Marriage Grows as More Americans Change Their Views," March 26, 2013, www .pewresearch.org/daily-number/support-for-same-sex-marriage -grows-as-more-americans-change-their-views/.

69 *Kennedy and Scalia quotes from* Obergefell v. Hodges: www .supremecourt.gov/opinions/14pdf/14-556_3204.pdf

71 *Senator Rubio's remarks*: "Rubio Delivers Address on 50th Anniversary of the 'War on Poverty,'" Marco Rubio, U.S. Senator for Florida, January 8, 2014, www.rubio.senate.gov /public/index.cfm/press-releases?ID=958d06fe-16a3-4e8e-b178 -664fc10745bf.

72 *Deportation*: Holly Avey, "It's Time for a Feminine Perspective," Human Impact Partners, November 24, 2014, www.humanimpact.org/tag/immigration/.

72 *Incarceration of black men*: Michelle Alexander, *The New Jim Crow: Mass Incarceration in the Age of Colorblindness* (New York: New Press, 2012).

72 *My Brother's Keeper*: David Hudson, "President Obama Launches My Brother's Keeper, His New Initiative to Help Young Men of Color," White House, February 27, 2014, www.whitehouse .gov/blog/2014/02/27/president-obama-launches-my-brothers -keeper-his-new-initiative-help-young-men-color.

THREE **Straight Camp**

82 *Recognizing gender*: Bobbi Carothers and H. T. Reis, "Men and Women Are from Earth: Examining the Latent Structure

of Gender," *Journal of Personality and Social Psychology*, October 22, 2012, advance online publication,www.psych.rochester .edu/people/reis_harry/assets/pdf/CarothersReis_2012.pdf.

84 *Women in film*: Melissa Silverstein, "Infographic: Women Directors in the Studio System," *Indiewire*, August 28, 2014, http://blogs.indiewire.com/womenandhollywood /infographic-women-directors-in-the-studio-system; Stacy L. Smith, Marc Choueiti, and Katherine Pieper, "Gender Inequality in Popular Films: Examining On Screen Portrayals and Behind-the-Scenes Employment Patterns in Motion Pictures Released between 2007–2013," University of Southern California, 2014, http://annenberg.usc.edu/pages/~/media /MDSCI/Gender%20Inequality%202007-2009.ashx; Sarah Kaplan, "Could the Sony Hacks Help Close the Hollywood Pay Gap?," *Washington Post*, January 11, 2015, www.wash ingtonpost.com/news/style-blog/wp/2015/01/11/could-the -sony-hacks-help-close-the-hollywood-pay-gap/.

85 *Naomi Wolf quote*: Naomi Wolf, *The Beauty Myth* (London: Chatto & Windus, 1990).

88 *Simone de Beauvoir quote*: Simone de Beauvoir, *The Second Sex*, trans. Constance Borde (New York: Vintage, 2011).

89 *Coco Chanel quote*: Lisa Chaney, *Coco Chanel: An Intimate Life* (New York: Penguin, 2012).

90 *Christine Lagarde quote*: As reported in *The Guardian*, "It's payback time: Don't expect sympathy—Lagarde to Greeks." Larry Elliott and Decca Aikenhead, May 25, 2012, www.the guardian.com/world/2012/may/25/payback-time-lagarde -greeks.

93 *On the word* bro: Katherine Connor Martin, "The History of 'Bro,'" Oxford Words Blog, October 9, 2013, http://blog.oxford dictionaries.com/2013/10/the-rise-of-the-portmanbro/; Erin Gloria Ryan, "The United States of Bros: A Map and Field Guide," *Jezebel*, April 2, 2014, http://jezebel.com/the-united-states-of-bros -a-map-and-field-guide-1550563737.

96 *Suicide*: Niobe Way, *Deep Secrets: Boys' Friendships and the Crisis of Connection* (Cambridge, MA: Harvard University Press, 2011); Centers for Disease Control and Prevention, "CDC Finds Suicide Rates among Middle-Aged Adults Increased from 1999–2010," press release, May 2, 2013, www .cdc.gov/media/releases/2013/p0502-suicide-rates.html; Shu-Sen Chang, David Stuckler, Paul Yip, and David Gunnell, "Impact of 2008 Global Economic Crisis on Suicide: Time Trend Study in 54 Countries," *British Medical Journal*, September 17, 2013, www.bmj.com/content/347/bmj.f5239.

98 *Aristotle quote*: Aristotle, *The Nicomachean Ethics*, trans. Martin Ostwald (New York: Prentice Hall, 1962).

99 *Overcompensation*: Robb Willer, Christabel Rogalin, Bridget Conlon, and Michael T. Wojnowicz, "Overdoing Gender: A Test of the Masculine Overcompensation Thesis," *American Journal of Sociology* 118 (2013): 980–1022; Norman Mailer, *Advertisements for Myself* (Cambridge, MA: Harvard University Press, 1992); Philip Roth, *Portnoy's Complaint* (New York: Vintage, 1994); Honoré de Balzac, *Treatise on Elegant Living*, trans. Napoleon Jeffries (New York: Wakefield, 2010).

104 *Susan Sontag quote*: Susan Sontag, "Notes on 'Camp'" in *Against Interpretation* (New York: Farrar, Straus and Giroux, 1966).

FOUR The Pornography Paradox

110 *Pornography numbers*: Sebastian Anthony, "Just How Big Are Porn Sites?," *Extreme Tech*, April 4, 2012, www.extremetech .com/computing/123929-just-how-big-are-porn-sites; "Pornhub 2013 Year in Review," *Pornhub Insights*, December 17, 2013, www.pornhub.com/insights/pornhub-2013-year-in-review.

111 *David Cameron quote*: "Online pornography to be blocked by default, PM announces," July 22, 2013, www.bbc.com/news /uk-23401076.

112 *Ruskin quote*: Tim Hilton, *John Ruskin* (New Haven, CT: Yale University Press, 2002).

118 Vanity Fair *quote*: Nancy Jo Sales, "Friends Without Benefits," *Vanity Fair*, September 26, 2013.

118 *Teenage sex*: Centers for Disease Control and Prevention, "Teenagers in the United States: Sexual Activity, Contraceptive Use, and Childbearing, 2006–2010. National Survey of Family Growth," Vital and Health Statistics, series 23, number 31, October 2011, www.cdc.gov/nchs/data/series/sr_23/sr23_031.pdf.

119 *Oral and anal sex*: National Survey of Sexual Health and Behavior, "Percentage of Americans Performing Certain Sexual Behaviors in the Past Year (N=5865)," table, www.nationalsexstudy.indiana.edu/graph.html.

119 *Sexual health*: Anjani Chandra, William D. Mosher, Casey Copen, and Catlainn Sionean, "Sexual Behavior, Sexual Attraction, and Sexual Identity in the United States: Data from the 2006–2008 National Survey of Family Growth," *National Health Statistics Reports*, March 3, 2001, www.cdc.gov/nchs/data/nhsr/nhsr036.pdf.

119 *Effects of pornography*: Dolf Zillmann and Jennings Bryant, "Effects of Massive Exposure to Pornography," in *Pornography and Sexual Aggression*, ed. Neil M. Malamuth (Orlando, FL: Academic Press, 1984); Drew A. Kingston, Paul Fedoroff, Philip Firestone, Susan Curry, and John Bradford, "Pornography Use and Sexual Aggression: The Impact of Frequency and Type of Pornography Use on Recidivism among Sexual Offenders," *Aggressive Behavior* 34.4 (2008): 341–51; Dominique Simons, Sandy Wurtele, and Peggy Heil, "Childhood Victimization and Lack of Empathy as Predictors of Sexual Offending against Women and Children," *Journal of Interpersonal Violence* 17.2. (2002): 1291–307; Timothy Benecke, "Male Rage: Four Men Talk About Rape," *Mother Jones*, July 1982, 22; Natalie Purcell, *Violence and the Por-*

nographic Imaginary (New York: Routledge, 2012); Todd D. Kendall, "Pornography, Rape, and the Internet," September 2006, http://idei.fr/sites/default/files/medias/doc/conf/sic/papers_2007/kendall.pdf; Berl Kutchinsky, "Pornography and Rape: Theory and Practice? Evidence from Crime Data in Four Countries Where Pornography Is Easily Available," *International Journal of Law and Psychiatry* 26 (1991): 47–64; Milton Diamond and Ayako Uchiyama, "Pornography, Rape, and Sex Crimes in Japan," *International Journal of Law and Psychiatry* 22.1 (1999): 1–22.

123 *Andrea Dworkin*: Andrea Dworkin, *Pornography: Men Possessing Women* (New York: Putnam's, 1981); Pornography Resource Center quote is from *Men Confront Pornography*, ed. Michael Kimmell (New York, Meridien, 1991); Andrea Dworkin, "Remembering the Witches," *Our Blood—Prophecies and Discourses on Sexual Politics* (London: Women's Press, 1982).

124 *Masturbation*: Jean Stengers and Anne Van Neck, *Masturbation: The History of a Great Terror* (New York: St. Martin's Press, 2001). The quotes from the below two books are taken from the book above: Thomas of Cantimpré, *Bonum Universale de Apibus*; Samuel-August Tissot, *Onanism*.

125 *Gail Dines quote*: Gail Dines, *Pornland: How Porn Has Hijacked Our Sexuality* (New York: Beacon, 2011).

126 *Pornography and intimacy*: M. Popovic, "Pornography Use and Closeness with Others in Men," *Archives of Sexual Behavior* 40.2 (2011): 449–56.

126 *Pornography and preexisting beliefs*: Paul J. Wright, "A Three-Wave Longitudinal Analysis of Preexisting Beliefs, Exposure to Pornography, and Attitude Change," *Communication Reports* 26.1 (2013): 13–25.

126 *Pornography and sexual development*: Fabien Saleh, Albert Grudzinskas Jr., Abigail Judge, *Adolescent Sexual Behavior in the Digital Age: Considerations for Clinicians, Legal Professionals and Educators* (Oxford, UK: Oxford University Press, 2014).

128 *My Little Pony pornography*: "My Little Porny: MLP Searches on Pornhub," July 22, 2015, www.pornhub.com/insights /pornhub-my-little-pony.

131 "After that came": Izabella St. James, *Bunny Tales* (New York: Running Press, 2009).

132 *Pornography and erotica*: Christine Cabrera and Amy Dana Menard, " 'She Exploded into a Million Pieces': A Qualitative and Quantitative Analysis of Orgasms in Contemporary Romance Novels," *Sexuality and Culture* 17.2 (2012).

138 *Diogenes in the marketplace*: Diogenes Laertius, *The Lives and Opinions of Ancient Philosophers*, trans. C.D. Yonge (London: Haddon and Sons, 1853).

140 *Dworkin "limp penis" and "patriarchy" quotes*: Andrea Dworkin, *"Remembering the Witches," Our Blood—Prophecies and Discourses on Sexual Politics* (London: Women's Press, 1982).

FIVE **Against Outrage**

148 *Carol Hanisch quote*: Carol Hanisch, "The Personal Is Political," *Notes from the Second Year: Women's Liberation* (New York: Radical Feminism, 1970).

154 *DiFranco quotes*: Hilary Crosley Coker, "Ani DiFranco Issues a Real Apology for Plantation Event," www.jezebel.com /ani-difranco-issues-a-real-apology-for-plantation-event -1493226658, January 14, 2014.

SIX **The Boys' Crisis, The Girls' Crisis**

164 *ADHD diagnosis*: Centers for Disease Control and Prevention, "New Data: Medication and Behavior Treatment," Attention-Deficit/Hyperactivity Disorder (ADHD), updated March 15, 2016, www.cdc.gov/ncbddd/adhd/data.html.

164 *Boys' crisis in academics*: Louann Brizendine, *The Male Brain* (New York: Broadway Books, 2010); J. Lee, W. Grigg, and P. Donahue, "The Nation's Report Card: Reading 2007, NCES 2007-496, 2007" (Washington, DC: U.S. Department of Education, National Center for Education Statistics, Institute of Education Sciences, 2007), table A-17; Michael Reichert and Richard Hawley, *Reaching Boys, Teaching Boys: Strategies That Work—and Why* (New York: Jossey Bass, 2010); National Center for Education Statistics, "Number of Students Suspended and Expelled from Public Elementary and Secondary Schools, by Sex, Race/Ethnicity, and State: 2006," table 169, http://nces.ed.gov/programs/digest/d10/tables/dt10_169.asp; National Center for Education Statistics, Thomas D. Snyder and Sally A. Dillow, *Digest of Education Statistics 2010*, NCES 2011-015 (Washington, DC: U.S. Department of Education, 2011), chapter 3, http://nces.ed.gov/pubs2011/2011015_3a.pdf.

166 *Michael Kimmel quote*: Michael Kimmel, "Solving the 'Boy Crisis,'" *Huffington Post*, April 30, 2013. www.huffingtonpost.com/michael-kimmel/solving-the-boy-crisis-in_b_3126379.html.

168 *Studies of gender differences*: Bobbi J. Carothers and Harry T. Reis, "Men and Women Are from Earth: Examining the Latent Structure of Gender," *Journal of Personality and Social Psychology*, advance online publication, October 22, 2012, www.psych.rochester.edu/people/reis_harry/assets/pdf/CarothersReis_2012.pdf; Madhura Ingalhalikar, Alex Smith, Drew Parker, Theodore D. Satterthwaite, Mark A. Elliott, Kosha Ruparel, Hakon Hakonarson, Raquel E. Gur, Ruben C. Gur, and Ragini Verma, "Sex Differences in the Structural Connectome of the Human Brain," in *Proceedings of the National Academy of Sciences of the United States of America*, ed. Charles Gross (Princeton, NJ: Princeton University Press, 2013).

169 *Judith Butler quotes*: Judith Butler, "Bodily Inscriptions, Per-

formative Subversions," in *Feminist Theory and the Body: A Reader* (New York: Routledge, 1999); Judith Butler, *Bodies That Matter* (New York: Routledge, 1993).

171 *Storm's gender*: Jayme Poisson, "Parents Keep Child's Gender Secret," *Toronto Star*, May 21, 2011, www.thestar.com/life /parent/2011/05/21/parents_keep_childs_gender_secret.html.

176 *Korean schools study*: H. Park, J. R. Behrman, and J. Choi, "Causal Effects of Single-Sex Schools on College Entrance Exams and College Attendance: Random Assignment in Seoul High Schools," *Demography* 50.2 (2013): 447–69.

177 *Toy preference*: Gerianne Alexander and Melissa Hines, "Sex Differences in Response to Children's Toys in Nonhuman Primates (*Cercopithecus aethiops sabaeus*)," *Evolution and Human Behavior* 23.6 (2002): 467–79; J. M. Hassett, E. R. Siebert, and K. Wallen, "Sex Differences in Rhesus Monkey Toy Preferences Parallel Those of Children," *Hormones and Behavior* 54.3 (2008): 359–64.

SEVEN **The Case for Living in Filth**

190 *Arlie Hochschild quote*: Arlie Hochschild, *The Second Shift: Working Families and the Revolution at Home* (New York: Penguin, 2012).

190 *Male and female housework participation*: Judith Treas and Sonja Drobnic, eds., *Dividing the Domestic: Men, Women, and Household Work in Cross-National Perspective* (Stanford, CA: Stanford University Press, 2010); Man Yee Kan, "Measuring Housework Participation: The Gap between 'Stylised' Questionnaire Estimates and Diary-based Estimates," *Social Indicators Research* 86.3 (2008): 381–400; S. Lee and J. Waite, "Husbands' and Wives' Time Spent on Housework: A Comparison of Measures," *Journal of Marriage and Family* 67.32 (2005): 328–36.

193 *Defining housework*: Katherine Ashenburg, *The Dirt on Clean* (Toronto: Vintage, 2008); Margrit Eichler and Patrizia Albanese, "What Is Household Work? A Critique of Assumptions Underlying Empirical Studies of Housework and an Alternative Approach," *Canadian Journal of Sociology* 32.2 (2007): 227–58.

195 *The economic value of housework*: Nancy Folbre, "Valuing Domestic Product," *New York Times*, May 28, 2012, http:// economix.blogs.nytimes.com/2012/05/28/valuing-domestic -product/.

200 *Gender stereotypes in housework participation*: Daniel Schneider, "Gender Deviance and Household Work: The Role of Occupation," *American Journal of Sociology* 117.4 (2012): 1029–72; *gender-typed housework*: Sabino Kornrich, Julie Brines, and Katrina Leupp, "Egalitarianism, Housework, and Sexual Frequency in Marriage," *American Sociological Review* 78.1 (2013): 26–50.

206 *Simone de Beauvoir quote*: Simone de Beauvoir, *The Second Sex*, trans. Constance Borde (New York: Vintage, 2011).

206 *The decline of housework*: Angela Davis, "The Approaching Obsolescence of Housework: A Working-Class Perspective," in *Women, Race and Class* (London: The Women's Press, 1981); Gail Collins, "Hillary's Next Move," November 10, 2012, *New York Times*, www.nytimes.com/2012/11/11/opinion/sunday /collins-hillarys-next-move.html?_r=0; *study of transgendered men*: Carla A. Pfeffer, "'Women's Work?': Women Partners of Transgender Men Doing Housework and Emotion Work," *Journal of Family and Marriage*, February 2010, 72:1, 165–83; Suzanne M. Bianchi, Melissa A. Milkie, Liana C. Sayer, and John P. Robinson, "Is Anyone Doing the Housework? Trends in the Gender Division of Household Labor," *Social Forces* 79.1 (2000): 191–228.

EIGHT **Messy Hope**

214 Illiad *quote*: Homer, *The Iliad*, trans. Robert Fitzgerald (New York: Farrar, Straus and Giroux, 1974).

215 *Simone de Beauvoir quote*: Simone de Beauvoir, *The Second Sex*, trans. Constance Borde (New York: Vintage, 2011).

217 *Marriage statistics*: D'vera Cohn, "Love and Marriage," Pew Research Center, February 13, 2013, www.pewsocialtrends .org/2013/02/13/love-and-marriage/; Wendy Wang and Kim Parker, "Record Share of Americans Have Never Married," Pew Research Center, September 24, 2014, www.pew socialtrends.org/2014/09/24/record-share-of-americans-have -never-married/.

218 *Family closeness*: "The Decline of Marriage and Rise of New Families: 1. Executive Summary," Pew Research Center, November 18, 2010, www.pewsocialtrends.org/2010/11/18 /the-decline-of-marriage-and-rise-of-new-families/.

218 *Hegel quote*: G. W. F. Hegel, *Outlines of the Philosophy of Right*, trans. Stephen Houlgate, Oxford World's Classics (Oxford, UK: Oxford University Press, 2008).

ACKNOWLEDGMENTS

S EVERAL early drafts of this book have appeared in various
magazines and newspapers. The *Atlantic* published a version of
chapter 1 under the title "The Masculine Mystique." The *New York
Times Sunday Review* published a version of chapter 7 under the title
"The Case for Living in Filth." *Esquire* has published stuff about the
death of my father and the new fatherhood, which later turned into
chapters 2 and 6. Chapter 3 about straight camp also came from work
I did for them. The chapter on pornography emerged out of an essay
that *Matter* magazine commissioned and then never ran. Still they
edited it beautifully, so I should thank them, I guess.

I am truly grateful to all the men and women who have helped
me: at the *New York Times*, Matt Sullivan and Trish Hall; at the
Atlantic, Scott Stossel and Kate Julian; at *Esquire*, Richard Dorment,
Tyler Cabot, Ross McCammon, and David Granger. David Granger
was more than an editor; he showed me how I could become the
writer who could write this book. Then there are the book people, who have forced this to become something more than another
bunch of essays cobbled together: PJ Mark at Janklow & Nesbit; my
female editor, Jennifer Lambert, at HarperCollins Canada; and my
male editor, Jofie Ferrari-Adler at Simon & Schuster. Gabe Gonda
gave me the title.

ABOUT THE AUTHOR

Stephen Marche is a novelist and culture writer whose work has appeared in *Esquire*, the *New York Times*, the *Atlantic,* and elsewhere. He lives in Toronto with his wife and children.